TOKYO
megacity

BY DONALD RICHIE

PHOTOGRAPHY BY BEN SIMMONS

TUTTLE PUBLISHING
Tokyo • Rutland, Vermont • Singapore

"This text is dedicated to the memory of Edward G. Seidensticker (1921-2007), the finest of Tokyo's chroniclers and the one who loved Tokyo best. He once said that the very shape of Tokyo ensured its many qualities. It is this shape that the text seeks to show, words in the shape of a city."—Donald Richie.

"These photographs are dedicated with the greatest respect to Donald Richie, Tokyo's esteemed "ambassador" and authority".—Ben Simmons.

We wish to sincerely thank Eric Oey, June Chong, Levi Christin, Bob Graham, Katharine Markulin Hama, Tim Porter, Kathryn Gremley, Reina Ogawa, Aya!, Keiko Odani, Rie, Rika & Tsuneko Nishimura, Ayako Ito, Rieko Eto & "Nagai," Shoi, Colleen & Oshin Sakurai, Deborah Collier, Rebecca Stockwell, Sarah Stuart Auman, Sarah S. Moon, Leza Lowitz and Linda Pringle for their kind support and invaluable encouragement.

Published by Tuttle Publishing, an imprint of Periplus Editions (HK) Ltd., with editorial offices at 364 Innovation Drive, North Clarendon, Vermont 05759 U.S.A. and 61 Tai Seng Avenue, #02-12, Singapore 534167

Library of Congress Cataloging-in-Publication Data
Richie, Donald.
  Tokyo : megacity / Donald Richie, text ; Ben Simmons, photographs .
    p. cm.
  Includes bibliographical references.
  ISBN 978-4-8053-0979-7 (hardcover)
1. Tokyo (Japan)--Pictorial works. 2. Tokyo (Japan)--Civilization. I. Richie, Donald, 1924- II. Title.
  DS896.35.S58 2010
  952'.135--dc22
                                        2009047760
ISBN: 978-4-8053-0979-7

Distributed by

North America, Latin America & Europe
Tuttle Publishing
364 Innovation Drive
North Clarendon, VT 05759-9436 U.S.A.
Tel: 1 (802) 773-8930; Fax: 1 (802) 773-6993
info@tuttlepublishing.com
www.tuttlepublishing.com

Japan
Tuttle Publishing
Yaekari Building, 3rd Floor, 5-4-12 Osaki
Shinagawa-ku, Tokyo 141 0032
Tel: (81) 3 5437-0171; Fax: (81) 3 5437-0755
tuttle-sales@gol.com

Asia Pacific
Berkeley Books Pte. Ltd.
61 Tai Seng Avenue #02-12
Singapore 534167
Tel: (65) 6280-1330; Fax: (65) 6280-6290
inquiries@periplus.com.sg
www.periplus.com

14 13 12 11 10   10 9 8 7 6 5 4 3 2 1

Printed in Singapore

TUTTLE PUBLISHING® is a registered trademark of Tuttle Publishing, a division of Periplus Editions (HK) Ltd.

Front endpapers An 1833 Hokusai print depicting the historic Nihonbashi Bridge and Mt. Fuji serves as a construction-site wall mural in the Nihonbashi district.

Page 1 A window-washing team hangs suspended over the city at the St. Luke Tower in the Tsukiji district.

Pages 2–3 The elegant steel girder construction of Tokyo Tower creates a distinct landmark, accentuated by illumination at the day's end.

Right *Sararimen* relax after work at a pub under the train tracks in Yurakucho.

Page 6 Graphically-illustrated coin lockers reflect the obsessive anime tastes prevalent in Akihabara.

CONTENTS

Foreword

ACCORDING TO THE 2008 United Nations Report on World Urbanization, Tokyo remains the largest city in the world, at its daytime peak containing 36 million people, considerably more than in all of California, more even than in all of Canada.

More too than double the size of such runners-up as Sao Paulo, Bombay, Mexico City, and New York. The city even finds its place (thirty-fifth) in the list of the world's largest countries. Yet, at the same time, Tokyo—true megalopolis though it be—is also ranked as one of the world's most livable cities, topped only by Copenhagen and Munich.

In a world where over-population appears a major threat, how does the world's largest city remain among the most livable, and for how long can it remain so? These are questions with many answers.

One of them would involve the very shape of the place, how it is made and how it grew. This shape was noticed, often with disapproval, by early Western visitors. Isabella Bird in 1880 said that Tokyo (formerly known as Edo) was a mere "aggregate of villages," and that as a city it "lacked concentration." In 1886, the American artist John La Farge was calling it "this big, dreary city of innumerable little houses." Later, in 1930, English author Peter Quennel was finding things no better—"a huge extension of a single neighborhood"—and in 1976 the sociologist David Riesman found Tokyo to be "a metropolis superimposed on a series of small villages."

These perceptions were noted and often echoed by the Japanese themselves. Novelist Abe Kobo wrote that the city is "a limitless number of villages. These villages and their people all appear identical. So no matter how far you walk, you seem to remain where you started, going nowhere at all." The mad old man of Tanizaki Jun'ichiro's last novel, referred to "that overturned rubbish heap of a Tokyo," and that finest of all Tokyo chroniclers, Nagai Kafu, wrote that " . . . it would seem that we Japanese are wholly lacking in the ability to build a city."

To build one, perhaps, but not to "grow" one. Though Edo/Tokyo was originally (like Washington, like Beijing) a city born by decree, a place with military intentions, the logical structure of the planned city shortly gave way to something more natural.

Clear winter atmospheric conditions reveal Mt. Fuji's distinctive peak rising dramatically beyond the skyscrapers of the Shinjuku District.

Preparation for the daily tuna auction is in full swing soon after sunrise at the Tsukiji Fish Market.

For planned, logical Edo to so quickly turn into unplanned, illogical Tokyo indicates that progress is in itself a dismantling, a destruction rather than a construction, one occasioned by practical needs. Architectural critic and city planner Lewis Mumford offers a paradigm.

"Those who refer to the winding streets of a town as mere tracings of the cowpath do not realize that the cow's habit of following contours usually produces a more economical and sensible layout than any inflexible system of straight streets." There was thus a strong social need not for one center but for many centers—these are the villages that make up Tokyo.

This "village" model is now disputed. Tokyo is not, it is said, just a congerie of villages, in that such units are not mere remnants of older social structures. Rather, they are more like cells of the body, continuing as vital social units.

Perhaps this organic structure might account for some of the livability of the city as a whole, in that it is so "natural." Each village-cell is composed of identical parts (nowadays the convenience store, the pachinko parlor, the karaoke place, no longer the rice store or the public bath) and, invariably, the *koban*, the station where your friendly neighborhood policeman works. Such "villages" take care of their own problems. Like cells in a body, each unit of this enormous conglomerate containing identical elements, the resulting pattern becomes organic—continuous, natural, all the parts fitting together in a harmonious way.

One can find echoed in this cell-like structure of Tokyo something equally cell-like in other cultural manifestations of the country. Traditional architecture, for example. Unit sizes are usually invariable. Your tatami mats would fit my floor, and my fusuma and shoji could become your doors and windows, and your pachinko parlor next door is just like mine.

As Kurt Singer, anthropologist extraordinaire, has said: "Let the Westerner sincerely try to live by Japanese customs "and he will instantly feel what a cell endowed with . . . human sensibility must be supposed to feel in a well-coordinated body." It is perhaps this "organic" quality in the construction of Tokyo that has contributed to its livability. A secure and comfortable warren is created, one which well suits the human animal. As the social critic Donald Olsen has observed: "If the domestic house is the microcosm of the city, so the city is the home writ large."

At the same time that we consider the spatial, however, we must also contemplate the temporal—the speed with which Tokyo mutates. It is common for a former resident to revisit an area and get lost because of all of the buildings torn down and

How does the world's largest city remain among the most livable?

The city combines the old and the new, is both traditional and trendy . . .

Fashionistas try for an evening snapshot of head designer Karl Lagerfeld outside the grand opening of the Ginza Chanel store.

all of the buildings put up in the interim. It has been said (by the Federation of Housing Production Organizations) that "private houses in Japan stand an average of 26 years before their owners knock them down and build anew."

Traditionally, buildings in this city have never lasted long. Edo would seem to have had more major fires than any similar metropolis. All the building materials (wood, wattle, plaster) were flammable. But they were also easily renewable. Wholesale reconstruction was as common as was wholesale destruction. Now, even though the building materials are glass, stone, and steel, the habit of routine reconstruction, pushed by the ever growing price of land (and the never ceasing demands of the construction industry) continues.

Perhaps Tokyo's livability lies also in the way the city accommodates itself to its citizenry, and not the other way about. Certainly, one can learn much about Tokyo by looking at those who live in it. These have been observed as industrious, wasteful, impatient, gregarious, lavish, enthusiastic, given to following the latest fads and to lamenting the past. They would seem to prove Jacques Rousseau's dictum that houses make a town but citizens make a city. Tokyo mirrors all their perceived qualities.

A further reason for Tokyo's livability might also be found in its chronology. It is a city of layers, of strata, in which the discrete units of the patchwork of villages that make its surface so varied are matched by the slices of the past that remain scattered on the face of the place. The city combines the old and the new, is both traditional and trendy, and these extremes define it.

It has been remarked that Tokyo's street pattern, despite social revolution, disaster, and time itself, has continued to resemble that of Edo, and architect Maki Fumihiko has demonstrated how contemporary Tokyo retains 19th-century Edo in the patterns of the winding streets. These remain basically unchanged, and the town-like groupings conforming to the topography remain true to Edo-period antecedents.

Anthropologist Jinnai Hidenobu finds that new forms are reset on inherited space, and that "developed as a modern city squarely atop this old structure, the essential features of Edo urban forms passed on unaltered." And if you want to know where the old vanished rivers, moats, and canals have gone, follow the elevated highways now set in their beds.

Architect Tange Kenzo believed that "everywhere you go in Tokyo, traditions and preferences of past generations—particularly those of the Edo period—exist side by side with Japanese preferences for the avant garde and for whatever is

A *Miko* Shrine Maiden passes gracefully through the Outer Shrine corridors of Meiji-Jingu Shrine.

chic." Thus, in Tokyo at its most modern, we will find attitudes, assumptions, preferences, and expressions the like of which we recognize from those of Edo. Even the kids shopping in Shibuya are displaying a commercial aesthetic we have seen before in old Asakusa.

To account for its shape and its history, Tokyo is commonly thought of as being divided into two major parts. These are what that eminent historian of the city, Edward Seidensticker, called Shitamachi, the "low city,"and Yamanote, the "high city." The former, built on the delta of the Sumida River, is what is left of yesterday—old Edo. The latter, built on surrounding higher ground, the hills leading to the Musashino Plain, is modern Tokyo, the world of today and perhaps tomorrow.

As the city expands, however, economic enterprise calls for a place of its own, and a third city has evolved. This might be called the "mid-city," someplace between the relatively old and the brand new, a place where the two for a moment mingle, where low city energy meets high city enterprise, where money can be made.

So, all together, megacity Tokyo looks like this: from the banks of the Sumida River spread what remains of the old city—defined by the Shitamachi Museum as composed of Kanda, Nihonbashi, Kyobashi, Ueno, Asakusa, Honjo, and Fukugawa. There we here find a temple or two from the Edo period (1615-1868), a bit more from the Meiji era (1868-1912), a little more from Taisho (1912-1926) and from Showa (1926-1989)—mainly what is left from the Kanto earthquake of 1923 and the fire-bombing of Tokyo in 1945—and lots from the present Heisei period (from 1989 on). Despite the quickening torrent of erosion, Tokyo remains in this sense nearly 600 years deep—older than New York.

Originally, it was simply the site of a local lord named Ota Dokan who built himself a modest castle in 1456. It was from this location that the city spread. Edo (the name translates as "bay door") was built largely on reclaimed land and what is now Ginza, Shimbashi, and Nihonbashi had been under water. The place-name of Hibiya, in mid-city Tokyo, means a place where seaweed was cultured. It was here that those who built Edo originally lived.

These people were brought in by Tokugawa Ieyasu, unifier of Japan, who decided that this would be the site of his new military capital. The place was mainly marsh and lacked drinkable water, but the warlord saw that this strip between the river and hills could be easily defended and that the port was protected from storms. So it was here that he fortified his castle,

Tokyo is commonly thought as being divided into "low city" & "high city."

This castle-city kept growing. There was never enough space.

The Rainbow Bridge across Tokyo Bay demonstrates its colorful name when illuminated at twilight. It connects downtown Tokyo with Odaiba.

dug moats and canals, and set up his shogunate.

The shogun's *daimyo* (retainers) built their residences here, and with them came their samurai warriors, followed by the carpenters, masons, fullers, weavers, dyers, cooks and footmen who created this new city. Nihonbashi became the administrative center of Japan, and it was from its central bridge (Nihonbashi means "Bridge of Japan") that all distances were to be officially measured.

The results were still to be viewed when the American scholar, W.E. Griffis, arrived in 1876. He observed that the general shape of old Edo was "that of an egg with the point to the south, the butt to the north, and the yolk of this egg is the castle."

This yolk, this core, is commonly thought of as unoccupied. But this is not quite true. Empty also means not filled with streets, buildings, nor people. For here, in the middle of the largest city in the world, is this wild park, this island of green—280 acres of it—said to be home to rabbits and pheasants as well as the Imperial family. The royals dwell there modestly with their Imperial household staff, living in a manner considerably less unostentatious than did the former tenants, the *bakufu*, the house and staff of the shogunate, the Tokugawa family.

By 1600, Tokugawa Ieyasu, leader of the clan and "unifier of Japan," had achieved a military hegemony. By the following year he had been named shogun and the construction of his castle was underway. It grew into a great city itself, the first of the city's many "cities within the city."

All the *daimyo* had to contribute. Lumber was levied, the great cyclopean stones still lining what is left of the Imperial moat were gathered. Some were so enormous that, shipped up the coast to growing Edo, only two of them would fit on a single boat and each and required 200 men to shift them. Pure white stucco, made from imported lime, was brought in to cover the outer walls, and specially-baked gray clay tiles constituted the roofs, with two enormous gold dolphins installed at the very summit.

And this castle-city kept growing. There was never enough space. This is why the lower hills were leveled, why the bay was pushed back and the land filled in. Eventually the whole area contained the largest castle in the world, holding, as it had to, the shogun and his entire cabinet and the *daimyo* and their retinues, which included not only their samurai, but also all of their attendants and their families. In addition there were the craftsmen and the servants, and then all the merchants and farmers who provided for them. Richard Cocks, one of the few

A mother leads her young daughters into Meiji Shrine to celebrate the annual *Shichi-Go-San* (7-5-3) ceremony, when children 7, 5 and 3 years of age visit Shinto shrines across the country in traditional kimono..

Westerners to have seen the place back then, wrote in 1616 that the castle was enormous—as large, he said, as the whole city of Coventry in England.

In a way, the castle became the architectural personification of an ideal feudalism—with the shogun at the apex of this pyramid of power—a structure that lasted the 15 generations of the Tokugawa family. But it did make something of a crowd.

The castle was filled to bursting—a whole harem of wives and concubines, dozens of *daimyo,* hundreds of samurai, thousands of servants and most with no place to live except, eventually, outside the walls in what became the new city of Edo.

By this time, however, the castle was no longer a fort. It did not need to be one. Ieyasu had conquered everyone, had engineered what has been called "an era of peace." Nonetheless, his palace remained imposing: 16 kilometers in circumference, 66 gates, 19 watchtowers. The roof of the main keep, 58 meters tall, was twice as tall as that surviving at Himeiji Castle. It did not, however, survive. Destroyed by fire in 1657, it was never restored due to the cost. Yet it was apparently a marvel.

Apparently, because there are few sketches, no drawings, no woodcut prints of the castle as it was. Its delineation was forbidden, its image taboo. This was official policy. The Tokugawa was a military hegemony, the longest lived the world has ever known. Though it no longer functioned as one, the palace was still a military secret. By now, however, it was completely dependent on the outside for food and water, and the samurai sat idle, no more wars to fight.

As the castle dwindled, Edo grew. Retainers moved away from the designed grid of *bakufu* power. The straight streets and square corners became convoluted as convenience called, as they were crossed by more expedient paths, by short cuts, as the purely military pattern became civilian, and then descended into that tangled geography so typical of the needs of free trade. It has been said that it was as though the monumental man-made geography of Washington, D.C. had, once past the White House, reverted to the paths and lanes of rural Virginia.

So it is here with this castle, now the imperial palace, that one should begin exploring Tokyo, that livable meglopolis. Then one goes down northeast to Shitamachi, the low city, where all those fullers and footmen lived; then up through the mercantile mid-city to the high-city hills where the ruler and his samurai were; and on to the burgeoning south-west, following the geography and the trail of history into the future.

From the banks of the Sumida River spread what remains of the old city . . .

The Imperial Palace

In the middle of the vast city of Tokyo lies the Imperial Palace, the castle grounds surrounded by its walls, moats, gates. It is the official residence of the Japanese Imperial family and even has a mailing address (1, 1-1, Chiyoda, Chiyoda-ku, Tokyo), yet its grounds also contain presumably primeval forests.

It has been compared to New York's Central Park and has been called the most expensive property in the world, its worth having been estimated as equivalent to the value of all the real estate in California.

It also constitutes one of the major obstacles to Tokyo traffic, trains, subways, trucks and cars, all these having to make long, crowded detours around it. But no one complains and no one is allowed in, though the pedestrian public can venture onto the inner palace grounds twice a year (January 2 and December 23) to give, respectively, New Year's greetings and best wishes on His Imperial Highness's birthday.

Otherwise, the visitor must be content with the single "view"— Nijubashi, a bridge backed by the Fushimi Tower, one of the few original buildings (first half of the 17th century), a view captured on the first Tokyo picture postcard ever printed, and seen on most ever since.

Because Tokyo was from the first a planned military capital, the palace and

its grounds have always constituted something of a Forbidden City. The last and largest of Japanese castles, Edo's towered over the Musashino plain, but did not last long. The main castle keep was destroyed by fire in 1657 and other parts of the castle have been burned a number of times—from the insurrections of 1868 to the U.S. fire bombings of Tokyo in 1945.

Otherwise, all that is left are a number of place names derived from where the enormous castle stood. Takebashi (Bamboo Bridge) where the Tokyo Museum of Modern Art

Above A stone bench makes a great spot to stop and admire the inner moat and waterfowl near the Imperial Palace's Sakuradamon Gate.
Right Dawn's first light warmly illuminates the Palace's Nijubashi Bridge, overlooked by the Fushimi Yagura Watchtower.

presently resides, Toranomon (Tiger Gate) now a part of mid-city Tokyo, and the Marunouchi district, facing Tokyo Station. It is from this center then that the city spread.

Above A stone lion, or *shishi*, statue stands guard outside the outer defensive walls of the Imperial Palace. Tradition dictates that a pair of *shishi*, one male and the other female, guard the entrances of buildings of importance, such as many temples and shrines.

Right The massive wooden gate at Yasukuni Shrine dwarfs a young boy in formal kimono.

Left An Imperial Watchtower contrasts with a modern office building. **Above** A young visitor feeds the white pigeons at Yasukuni Shrine.

Below A white swan glides through the famous 'double bridge' refection of Nijubashi Bridge.

Below The statue of Ota Dokan, the samurai architect who designed and built Edo Castle in 1457, faces the Imperial Palace from inside the modern laminated-glass and steel structure of the Tokyo International Forum.
Bottom Rowboats await punters visiting the Chidorigafuchi Moat at the Imperial Palace.

Above People take boats out in Chidorigafuchi, the north-eastern moat of the Imperial Palace, to enjoy a bit of respite in the otherwise bustling heart of the city. April, when the stately cherry trees (*sakura*) are in full bloom, is a particularly popular time for such outings.

Right Sakurada Gate at the Imperial Palace. Visitors may enter the Imperial Palace on only two days each year.

THE LOW CITY

The Low City, build on the delta of the Sumida River, is what is left of old Edo.

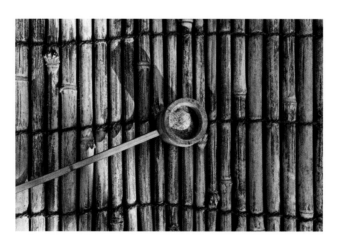

Above A handcrafted bamboo ladle rests on the simple bamboo and rope cover of
a water basin at Toshogu Shrine, located inside Ueno Park.
Right A Buddhist monk patiently awaits alms from passersby while chanting on
Chuo Dori Avenue near Ueno Station.

THE LOW CITY

Just as Edo was traditionally divided into the high city on one hand and the low city on the other, so the inhabitants are thought of as classified into the samurai class (aristocratic) and the plebian (commoner) class—with perhaps the merchant class forming a kind of mid-class in between.

Class differences, based on Confucian concepts imported from China, were strongly reinforced during the reign of the *bakufu,* the Tokugawa shogunate's government. Whatever its other virtues, such doctrine creates a malable populace, easy to intimidate and to control. Early Edo was like a military camp.

Status, rank, was everything and the resulting classes were to be defined and separated. Everyone was to have his or her place, and there was no leaving it. Samurai must live apart from merchants, craftsmen were to be assigned housing by trade, farmers stayed on the farm, and travel permits were needed to visit even neighboring provinces.

Officially, the most powerful and privileged were the samurai and their *daimyo* leaders. Beneath them was ranked the peasant class, though in actuality the farmers had little power. Nonetheless, as in most militaristic societies, "the people" were offered official respect. Beneath them were the artisans and at the very bottom (though above the various proscribed classes) were the merchants. Though this lowly merchant class eventually controlled much of the country's cash and many a samurai was in debt to many a wealthy merchant, as a social category this class was officially denied the power and privilege that it actually held.

Given such top-down cultural control, it is not surprising that Edo's class structure should have emerged in the strata-like formation still culturally visible. The pyramid looked like this: On top, the samurai (*shi*), just under this, the farmers (*no*), below them the artisans (*ko*) and near the bottom, the merchants (*sho*).

The upper layer (samurai culture) contains many of those traditional things that foreigners now associate with Japaneseness: the formal kimono, official architecture, fine

calligraphy, the *Noh* drama, *ikebana* flower arranging, almost all of the martial arts, and much more. This could be called the official culture of the high-city folk.

Contrasted to this would be that of the people of the low city. These would have been the artisans (and, increasingly, the merchant class), since peasants by definition are not credited with having much culture at all.

Low-city culture was also traditional to the extent that here were created many of the objects of daily use: tools, utensils, pottery, lacquer work, fabrics, etc. At the same time, however, since these were all for sale, there was a cultural current visible in the low-city, a continual infusion of the new—including new money— which was perhaps lacking in high-city culture.

From our point of view, most "samurai" culture is now stationary, petrified, though often very beautiful. Low city culture, however, was initially the home of change, and remains so, even now, despite the fact that the *Shitamachi* itself appears old-fashioned.

The reason for the contemporary continuation of low-city vitality is that it now informs the whole of the city, indeed, the whole of the country. Though its most famous early products—the kabuki, the wood-block print, the various folk festivals—now seem just as traditional as anything that the aristocratic high-city culture produced, there is a difference.

To understand this one might look at the evolution of low-city culture. It is a continuing process. New and hopefully

"improved" models constantly appear, distribution outlets are arranged, advertising is addressed, fashions push the product, and profits can be made.

At the same time, the popular arts exhibit no conservative urge to retain the time-honored or to respect any perceived integrity in the original. Here is an aesthetic example: The rules for fine calligraphy (much esteemed in high-city Edo) were not relaxed and, indeed, still aren't. In the "better" parts of Tokyo, a fine calligraphic hand is still considered an indication of a sterling character. In low-city Edo, an accomodation of standards was the rule. When color-saturated if oily aniline paints were imported from abroad, most *ukiyo-e* printmakers adopted them without a qualm, even though this meant dropping the time-honored vegetable-based colors.

Change is always with us. The popular arts are always vital and it is this vitality that keeps them popular. There is thus a continual tide of the new that, frivolous as it often is, agitates the culture that produces it because it is this that is salable.

There is another factor also to be considered when contemplating low-city Edo culture. When something is forbidden an appetite for it is created. In the military atmosphere of Edo—one we might now consider, with its various sumptuary laws, a near police-state—citizens were attracted to such alternatives.

Edo scholar Nishiyama Matsunosuke has indicated how the principles of warrior rule governed the rank or status of individuals and families in the feudal hierarchy. His examples are all from the *daimyo* level. "Social rank determined the shape and size of the Edo residence, the kind of vehicles, furnishing, and clothing he was allowed. Distinctions included the colors and designs of clothing . . . even the borders of the *tatami* in Edo castle varied according to the rank of the officials who sat on them."

If proscriptions were this severe at the top of the social pyramid, one may imagine what it was like for those at the bottom. Everything was to be indicative of ranking: hair styles, length of kimono sleeves, the colors permitted, the right to two swords, to one sword, to none. And not only was the recommended enforced, but innovations were forbidden.

One result was that Edo popular culture (as distinguished from official culture) based itself firmly upon the proscribed. The new product, the latest import, was searched out. Fashion was based on what was worn in the licensed quarters of the city: a certain color worn by a courtesan, a new way of tying one's sash by an actor; woodblock prints made the likenesses of geisha and sumo athletes alike known to all and eligible for imitation; the outlawed and otherwise proscribed were often the heroes of the kabuki.

Another result was the inordinate attraction of the *shin hatsubai,* the "new product." It still demands much attention in the media—and the parade of popular enthusiasms which stretch all the way from the Edo period until now: beige-striped kimono material, the craze for ornamental rabbits, the yo-yo, the hula-hoop, the *tamagochi* simulated pet, and on to the latest in cell phones and i-pods.

Nishiyama goes on to tell us that the strength of this low city culture lay "in its spectacular breadth and diversity." Even the general public took part in leisure pursuits as best it could and played an active role in the creation of new cultural forms.

This public formed the bulk of the population of Edo (by 1780 estimated at one million at a time when London held only two-thirds of that) and formed a new category, the *chonin,* a term often translated as townspeople. They were initially there to serve the needs of the samurai, but in time developed needs of their own. There were certainly more of them. Over half of this million living in Edo were some kind of *chonin.* Many were poor, but many were getting richer. This included the growing merchant class.

In fact the term *chonindo* ("the way of the merchants") was heard as frequently as *bushido* ("the way of the warrior.") Tales

were told of rich but socially inferior merchants who lined their kimono with precious brocade, though outwardly exhibiting only the prescribed colors they were traditionally obliged to wear.

Though what we would now call their lifestyle was regulated by various sumptuary laws, and conspicuous extravagance was supposed to bring summary punishment, wealthy *chonin* lived in a way unthinkable for not only the average citizen but for most samurai as well. At the same time, this low-city culture presumed an ideal much at odds with that of the stern Confucian castle in the middle of the city. It was seditious, though its subversive intent was disguised.

In the same manner, other offenses against official decorum

Above from left to right Tuna is arranged for auction just after sunrise at the Tsukiji Fish Market (extreme left). A graceful visitor admires the cherry blossoms at Koishikawa Korakuen Gardens (second from left). A lotus water lily plant is sprinkled with raindrops from a summer shower at Shinobazu Pond in Ueno Park (third from left). Sumida River fireworks glimpsed from Kaminarimon Gate in Asakusa (second from right). The vermilion-colored Tsutenkyo Bridge arches gracefully over a small tributary inside Koishikawa Korakuen, an Edo Period garden (extreme right). **Bottom left** A statue of Matsuo Basho (Japan's most renowned haiku poet) overlooks the Sumida River and Kiyosubashi Bridge from the Basho-An Garden.

were described as mere fashion. In the *Shitamachi*—particularly in the popular plazas at either end of the Ryogoku Bridge, in the pleasure grounds of Asakusa, and in the licensed quarters of the Yoshiwara—life was not the stretch of hard labor prescribed by the authorities. Rather, the ideal was drifting as elegantly as possible along life's river, free (in the words of an Edo poet) "as a gourd floating downstream," a part of the *ukiyo,* the floating world.

An attitude cultivated among merchants and artisans was known as *iki,* a term which we might variously translate. "Cool" comes close, it suggests being "with it" and the Japanese term incorporates an assumed insouciance that refused to assign any particular importance to the stern edicts from the castle. To be sure, the castle was where the power was. Peasant uprisings were put down with brutality, and the kabuki is still full of stories of what happens to those who got caught—often young lovers mating across the social gap and ending up as double suicides.

Samurai were forbidden the pleasures of the pleasure-quarters and were subject to discipline if apprehended. The problem was solved when a special kind of hood-like headgear was put on sale. By purchasing and wearing one of these, the errant aristocrat indicated that he was incognito. This was a very low-city-like solution, one which satisfied the aristocrats and the authorities as well.

The authorities themselves were not immune to the charms of this proscribed popular culture. The novelty-loving shogun, Tsunayoshi, in 1682 went to see the first Korean circus to come to Japan. When an enormous whale beached itself in Shinagawa in 1798, the whole carcass was considered so exotic that it was lugged into the gardens of the palace to be examined by the upper classes.

Thus, culture high and low early merged in Edo and the result informs the distinctive flavor of Tokyo even now. There are, in actuality, two Japans. There is the "official" version (tea ceremony, subservient kimono-clad women) which is also the exported version and the one shown visitors. It is also the way that Japanese society likes to view itself, whether or not it happens to be accurate.

Then there is the other Japan, one which might be called the "real" one. Its people, as has have been often noted, do not behave like "Japanese" because none of the rules of order and decorum insisted upon by the official version apply. And example might be the people shown in the comedies of *kyogen*,

in the wood-block caricatures of the Edo period, or—in our own time—those shown in pop-lit, in manga cartoons, and in the works of filmmaker Imamura Shohei.

These people, almost always from the lower classes, do not recognize the meaning of fidelity or loyalty, they are completely natural and are to that extent "uncivilized" if civilization means (as it does) an avoidance of the natural.

Imamura himself said that "I happen to be more interested in the Japan that flourished before the artistic decadence

fostered by political isolation in the feudal period," later adding: "The Japanese did not change as a result of the Pacific War . . . they haven't changed in thousands of years."

The traditional arts and crafts still maintain, as does the old castle and the ancient shrine. Equally there, however, is a taste for the new, the inclination for the transient, the insouciant reverence (to coin an oxymoron) that still so distinguishes this city. This is the spirit of *matsuri*—devotion, novelty, fun.

When the social pattern shifted (in the late 1850s), the pyramid of power was, as it were, turned upside down, and the rich and formerly despised *chonin* merchant turned up on top of the pile, where he still remains.

Commoners were allowed to take surnames, to intermarry with other classes, and to wear clothes once exclusive to the samurai class. An edict allowed, and then required, the samurai to cut off their trademark top-knots. Then there was an edict banning the wearing of swords except on plainly ceremonial occasions.

This was the result of the decay of the Shogunate, the restlessness of some of the *daimyo,* and the sudden appearance of the American commodore, Matthew Perry, and his fleet of black ships. To American eyes, "Japan fell asleep in the reign of Queen Elizabeth and awoke in the reign of Queen Victoria" In actual fact, however, no one was asleep and Japan was forging what we now know as its traditional culture.

Above from left to right *Koi* (carp) appear to swim inside delicate hand-painted laquerware bowls on a reed tray (extreme left). A vendor cooks fresh fish over charcoal at a traditional summer street fair (second from left). Businessmen in conservative dark suits stroll beneath maple trees in bright autumn colors at Koishikawa Korakuen Gardens (third from left). An elevated expressway and a fat-moving couple cross the Nihonbashi Bridge (upper third from right). A traditional costume is worn with fashionable flair at Asakusa's Sanja Festival (second from right). Commuter trains swing around the tracks curving into Ueno Station (far right). **Opposite bottom** A dancer shares a smile at Asakusa's Samba Festival.

However, as we have seen, everything changed after 1868, the beginning of the Meiji period. People began to read print from left to right (rather than the opposite, or up to down); chairs were introduced into government offices, shoes became popular—particularly if they announced their modernity by squeaking. They could even be induced to do so if one purchased and inserted specially made straps of "singing leather." In addition, traditional court dress shifted from kimono to Western suits, ladies followed with flounces and bustles, people were encouraged to eat beef, the coffee shop took the place of the tea house, and beer began to replace saké.

There were many reasons for such change but one of them is that change costs money and the *chonin* had most and wanted more. From now on, Japanese culture would be defined mainly by mercantile fact. It still is.

Asakusa

Asakusa, the core of old Shitamachi, got its name from an account of early Edo stating that the grass there was short—*asa* meaning "short" and *kusa* meaning "grass." This area was northeast of the site of the shogun's castle, an unlucky direction and perhaps the reason for the shorter grass. To temper evil influences, a temple was built in 1590 by the first shogun, Tokugawa Ieyasu.

Properly called Senso-ji, the place is popularly known as the Asakusa

Kannon Temple, named after the Buddhist "goddess of mercy," a small golden replica of whom was providentially found at just the place chosen for the temple.

With all the worshippers gathering there, Asakusa became a major entertainment district, eventually boasting the Opera House (an all-girl revue), Japan's largest merry-go-round, the Denkikan, Japan's first (1903) movie theater, and the country's largest red-light district right next door.

Old Asakusa vanished in the U.S. fire bombings of 1945, during which some 80,000 people were killed and some

two-fifths of the city was destroyed. The Kannon Temple was hit on March 9th, and was consumed in two hours.

The present temple (ferro-concrete) was inaugurated only in 1950. By this time, however, Tokyo was expanding toward the west, away from Asakusa and the low city. As money moved elsewhere, efforts were made to profitably gentrify the place—olde Nippon plastic cherry blossoms, *jinrikisha* (rickshaws) pulled about by local youths, the Nakamise, grand entrance to the temple grounds, given over to tourist kitsch.

Now the venerable Rokku (once six blocks of drama, sword fights, and motion-picture palaces) is calling itself The Rox, the Denkikan Mansions are seeking to distinguish themselves as "living units for the really discerning," and such flashy façade slogans as "Beaux Arts: We Sell a Tasty Life," now beckon.

To no avail. Asakusa is no longer the core of a vibrant popular culture. Except for when the Sunday racetrack results are posted, and during the Sanja Festival (late May), Asakusa remains a reminder of Tokyo in earlier days. As for true pop culture, it moved West and we will meet it again at a better address—Harajuku.

Everyone pitches in during Asakusa's Sanja Festival in the Spring (**top left**). The great Kaminarimon Thunder Gate marks the entrance to the narrow and often crowded Nakamise shopping street, which leads directly to Senso-ji Temple (**right**).

Above A young fellow grilling *ika* (squid) is one of numerous vendors surrounding Senso-ji, better known as Asakusa Kannon Temple, during the holiday season.
Right The distinctive architecture of Asahi Beer's headquarters is a well-known landmark in the Asakusa area.

Below Women join in to help carry their neighborhood's *mikoshi* portable shrine during the Sanja Festival in May.

Left A young *jinrikisha* driver checks her schedule while waiting for customers on Kaminari-mon Avenue in Asakusa. **Below** Masterpiece tattoos are revealed during the heat of the Sanja Festival.

Near right There is method in the madness of the scrum guiding their *mikoshi* (portable shrine) through the crowded lanes towards Senso-ji Temple. **Middle right** Stylishly-coiffed women in traditional costume lend their support during Sanja. **Far right** A beautifully sculpted bronze *Nadebotoke* (Rubbing Buddha) statue attracts worshippers hoping for good health to Senso-ji.

Left *Yakatabune* excursion houseboats slowly cruise the Sumida River near Asakusa Park during the peak cherry blossom season in April.
Right New Year's is a popular time to seek good fortune at Senso-ji Temple. Like this young woman, many people in Japan record their wishes on paper and tie them to racks at temples and shrines throughout the country.

Ueno

Tokyo has a number of public parks, although London has 12 times more. Among these, Ueno Park is the largest, and ranks among the oldest. It is believed that the waves of what is now Tokyo Bay originally lapped these shores, that they came right up to where both the park and Ueno Station now stand, and that the Shinobazu Pond in the south of the park is what is left of one of its inlets.

The grounds were taken over by the temples and then by governmental patronage, and only in 1873 was the area declared a public park.

It grew to contain the first art museum in Japan, the first zoo, and Ueno station itself became for Tokyo what the Gare du Nord is for Paris, a gateway from the north.

Now the park holds five major museums, a panda family, and such places from the past as the Tosho-gu Shrine (1651, now listed as a National Treasure) as well as the bright red hill-side Kannon-do, built in imitation of Kyoto's Kiyomizu temple and the oldest of Ueno's old buildings (1631).

Not so old but just as beautiful is the lotus-filled Shinobazu Pond, with its octagonal temple of the goddess Benten on its ornamental island—a copy since the original was burned in the Tokyo fire-bomb raids and restored (ferro-concrete) only in 1958. The pond itself had become a rice paddy during WWII

and postwar it was threatened by developers interested in building a massive car park. These ambitions thwarted, Ueno remains the Tokyo home of the tranquil lotus and the migrating duck.

Adjacent to the park is the last of the old public markets, *Ameyoko-cho,* a postwar black-market warren now bristling with cut-rate brand names and old-style seafood-mongers, the latter selling what is purported to be the cheapest fish in town.

Here, in the market, one sees perhaps the last of the *Edokko,* those "children of old Edo," whom one account has called: open, generous, hot-tempered, inquisitive, quick to offense and quick to forget—few of which traits are now associated with the

Above A tunnel of vermilion-colored wooden *torii* gates offers a private moment inside Ueno Park.
Right Benten-do Temple, on its small island, is almost hidden in the mist of a summer storm sprinkling rain on the lotus water lilies of Shinobazu Pond in Ueno Park.

contemporary Japanese. To qualify, an *Edokko* must boast that both parents and all four grandparents were born in the *Shitamachi,* preferably Kanda but Ueno will do.

Left Young girls consult their cellphones on the steps of the Gallery of Horyu-ji Treasures at the Tokyo National Museum, located inside Ueno Park. **Below** Visitors throng Benten-do Temple during the cherry blossom season in April.

Left Travelers take a break inside Ueno Station.
Right A close view reveals the fine detail in a handcarved dragon with goldleaf on a wooden gate at Tosho-gu Shrine, located inside Ueno Park.
Below Revelers fill Ueno Park during the brief but beautiful peak of the cherry blossoms in April.

Above A young enthusiast visits a special district packed with motorcycles and motorcycle accessory shops in Ueno.

Below Vendors hawk their wares from a multitude of open-front shops as potential customers surge through the narrow *Ameyoko* market street, Tokyo's last surviving public market.

Above A couple enjoy the view of Benten-do Temple from inside a cafe on the shore of Shinobazu Pond during a summer rain.

Right An airship passes above the five-story Ueno Pagoda (built in 1639 at Kanei-ji Temple), located inside Ueno Park.

Akihabara

That section of downtown Tokyo, named after the Akiba Shrine that once stood here amid empty fields, is now ablaze with electronics and is presently calling itself "Electric City." The soubriquet is fitting because Akihabara has long been more associated with commerce than with religion.

Originally a neighborhood where craftsmen lived, it early on (1890) got its own railway station and opened itself up to commerce. It first busied itself with domestic goods, then during the war years it was bicycles, then radios, and for a time it was rival to Ueno's *Ameyoko-cho* in the black-market trade.

Akihabara is still a market but now a much more massive and absolutely legal one. It specializes in consumer electronics and home appliances. Here, it has been said, the electronically sophisticated person can find anything that has ever been invented. Here too are the best-sellers among anime movies and the latest in video games.

About 600 electronics shops are crowded into less than three square kilometers, all of them selling the latest gizmos and gadgets. The resultant popularity (annual sales of ¥30 trillion, some ten percent of all domestic electronic sales) has made Akihabara wealthy enough to finance a major architectural face-lift and, as one guidebook has it, "become to electronics as Las Vegas is to gambling."

Thus, though officially a part of the low city, Akihabara has come to look very high-city in its affluence and customer-orientation. It has even bred a new kind of customer—the *otaku*, that single-minded, sometimes obsessive geek who will buy practically anything connected to a favorite video game or a beloved anime character. The new affluence and the increasing youth of these customers have created such anime-esque Akihabara-inspired novelties as "maid cafes," where girls in aprons and skirts feed boys, and "butler cafes," where it is the other way about.

At the same time, electronic parts, spilling out into the street, filling up the boxes and buckets lining the shop fronts, make the place look very Asian. If, instead of plugs and sockets and computer chips, these were mangos and betelnuts, this would be transparent.

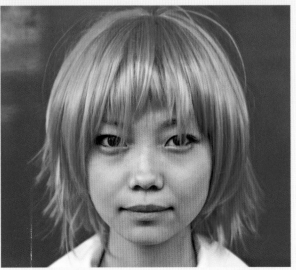

Above Even coin lockers are covered with anime fantasy characters in Akihabara.

Far left The multi-story Yodobashi Akiba electronics store in Akihabara attracts technology aficianados from all over Japan.

Left A young girl with blue hair on Chuo-dori Avenue fits right in . . . in Akihabara.

Above Flashing signs, passing traffic, and trains streaking by overhead create a dynamic twilight scene in Akihabara, "Electric City."

Left A stylish young woman chats on her cellphone while waiting to cross Chuo-dori Avenue in Akihabara.

Opposite top Cute young girls working at Popopure Maid Cafe wear French maid's uniforms and permanent smiles.

Opposite below left Young women in anime-inspired fashions try their luck with Akihabara sidewalk vending machines.

Opposite bottom right Two young women wait for a train under a billboard of two female anime characters.

Yanaka

Yanaka means "in the valley," and that is where this district is, lying between the heights of Ueno and the slopes of Hongo. Yanaka's position determined its future. Low lying, it avoided both the destruction of the 1923 Kanto earthquake and the incineration of that great 1945 conflagration, the fire-bombing of Tokyo.

Salvation occurred, some said, because the wind was blowing in a direction favorable to the place; others said that it was the result of there being over seventy local temples and almost as many graveyards (the largest, the Yanaka Reien, hosts some seven thousand graves), thus prompting Buddha's benevolence.

A result is that Yanaka, together with neighboring Nezu and Sendagi, retain what little is left of traditional residential Tokyo: narrow streets, old wooden houses (including an Edo-style *nagaya* "long house" or two), open-front shops, flower-filled window boxes, and no automobiles.

It remains one of the most livable sections of Tokyo, with lots of greenery, low rents (at least compared to Roppongi's), intact neighborhoods, many small shops, a true hamlet ambiance. It is also one of the best preserved sections of village-Tokyo and staunchly holds its own against the march of progress.

For all these reasons it has long been a favorite residence of the literati. The house where Natsume Soseki wrote *I Am a Cat* still stands, and the home of the author Mori Ogai is now part of an otherwise concrete hotel. Down the street is where the famous painter, Yokoyama Taikan, lived, the house presently a museum. There is also the atelier of sculptor, Asakura Fumio, a memorial to the aesthete Okakura Teishin, author of *The Book of Tea*, and—nowadays—a number of gentrified art galleries.

Nearby Nezu has its famous Nezu Shrine (1705), in the spring filled with the finest azaleas in all Tokyo. It is,

Above In the early morning, a young Shinto *kannushi* priest sweeps a gravel path in the azalea garden before visitors arrive at Nezu Shrine.

Right Spring visitors stroll the hillside azalea garden during a fine mid-April afternoon at Nezu Shrine.

however, no longer next door to one of the most famous of the red-light districts. This was forcibly moved to Susaki, back down along the river. This was done because Tokyo University is just up the hill and, as historian Edward Seidensticker has noted, "the proximity was not thought appropriate since the young men of the university were the future of the nation."

Top A tunnel-like row of Shinto *torii* gates borders the hillside azalea garden at Nezu Shrine.
Above Traditional earthern walls topped with ceramic tiles can still be found in Yanaka.
Right This venerable old family specialty shop offers *osembe* crackers in Sendagi.
Left Quiet sidestreets in old downtown Yanaka shelter tiny, carefully-tended gardens at traditional wooden residences, where *sudare* bamboo screens afford both privacy and shade.

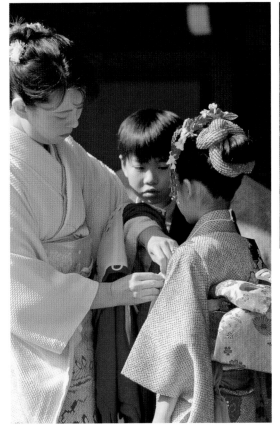

Left A family enjoys a seasonal visit to Nezu Shrine.
Above An attendant waters the Goten-no Suitei Garden inside the central courtyard of the Asakura Choso Museum in Yanaka, which commemorates the work of Japan's Rodin, Fumio Asakura (1883-1964).

Kanda

Among the qualifications for being an *Edokko* (and thus embodying the old *Shitamachi* spirit) were being third generation in the low city and having been born and raised in Kanda.

There is some confusion, however, in separating just which sections of the city belong to the low city and which to the high. Kanda is such an example. Since it is north of the castle, it was originally thought to be what we would call low city. Its earlier inhabitants were the fullers and footmen who worked at the castle, and later Kanda residents were said to be industrious, cheerful and noisy—at least, compared to the those who lived in the more staid high city.

And it had such traditional landmarks as the Kanda Myojin Shrine,

founded in 730, the present building reproducing the style of the 1616 reconstruction, though in concrete. It still has one of the three most famous traditional festivals in the city, and is still a proper place to begin a marriage.

Slowly, however, the modern moved in as the high city nudged nearer. Exotic Nikolai Cathedral, a Russian Orthodox place of devotion, was put up not far from Kanda Myojin. Novelist Tanizaki Junichiro, then a boy, watched it go up in 1890. Here this child of the low city first detected, as he put it, "the scent of the West."

With Westernization came higher education. Kanda eventually had the greatest concentration of private higher schools in the country with its three important universities: Meiji, Nihon, and Chuo. With these came not only students and teachers but also intellectual enquiry and lots of books. Kanda's main avenue at the Jinbocho crossing is still lined with bookstores, everything from antiquarian treasures to the latest in pop manga collections.

Kanda still maintains its marginal nature. To be an *Edokko*, you still ought to be third generation, born in Kanda. The venerable (if presently contro-versial) Yasukuni Shrine is just up the street, but at the same time Kanda itself is now next door to Otemachi, the entrance to the new mid-city, with its banks, bustle and big businesses.

Above Book lovers browse through the stalls of numerous used-booksellers in Kanda-Jimbocho.
Right Excursion houseboats and fishing boats line the Kanda River.
Opposite A Buddhist monk in a simple bamboo hat and plain black robes stands on the street in the Kanda to receive alms.

Far left A young couple wear formal kimono in a wedding ceremony at Kanda Myojin Shrine. **Near left** Nikolai-do Cathedral is the center of the Russian Orthodox Church in Japan. **Below left** Crews prepare *yakatabune* houseboats for evening excursions on the Sumida River and Tokyo Bay. **Right** Kanda Institute of Foreign Languages is a popular school near Kanda Station. **Below** A wedding party poses for a photograph in front of the main hall at Kanda Myojin Shrine.

Fukagawa

Early foreign visitors called Edo 'the Venice of Japan.' Rivers and canals were the thoroughfares of the city, and on these sailed the boats and ferries of the old capital. And nowhere were there more of these waterways than in Fukagawa, a town that lay between the city's two main rivers, the Sumidagawa and the Arakawa.

Along with the boats swam a large population of turtles, those creatures preferring the amphibious home that Fukagawa offered. So numerous were these that, when the famous print-maker Hiroshige wanted to picture Fukagawa in his views of Edo, he inserted not only the river and the boats, but also a large turtle.

Frogs abounded as well. The most famous of these, that written about by the haiku poet known by his pen-name, Matsuo Basho (1644-1694), was the frog that jumps into the ancient pond and contrasts all that stillness with the plop of his dive. One can find the poem itself carved in stone on a tablet not far from Basho's reconstructed cottage on the banks of the river.

It is at the rear of the Kiyosumi Teian Park, originally the garden of a wealthy merchant, eventually bought, in 1878, by the founder of the Mitsubishi empire. He donated it to Tokyo in 1932. It was designated one of the city's official "Scenic Beauty Spots" in 1979, and still offers some idea of what Fukugawa was once like.

The past lingers elsewhere as well. Monzen-naka-cho is a functioning temple town and Kiba still has its floating lumber stocks, though there are not many other tangible remains. The reason is the firebombing of Tokyo.

The dead from the initial attack were estimated at around 80,000, and there were ten more nights of bombing after that. Over 15 square miles of the city were burned, and nearly 300,000 buildings destroyed. The fires were so hot that the rivers boiled, as did those

Above Carp and turtles swim along the Isowatari Stepping-stone Path at Kiyosumi Teien Park. **Below left** A tugboat pushes a barge down the Sumida River.

Above right A local resident in a sunbonnet fishes from the old bridge on Tsukijima Island. **Right** Twilight traffic illuminates the Kiyosubashi Bridge as it passes over the Sumida River.

thousands who in them sought escape from the flames.

In these raids all of Fukagawa vanished. Except for a corner here and there, all of the present-day place is postwar. Yet Kiyosumi Park has been reconstructed, the temple town is thriving, and there are now turtles and frogs in the river.

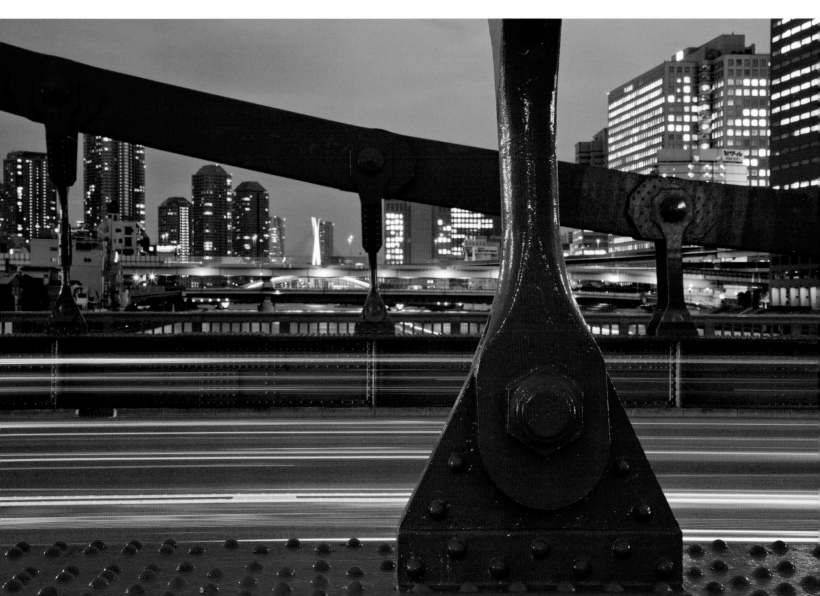

Opposite top The Ryotei Teahouse extends out over the pond at Kiyosumi Teien.
Opposite bottom A long, curving tunnel of flowering *hagi* (Lespedeza) greenery leads the way deeper into Mukojima-Hyak-kaen Gardens.

Right A businessman seeking good fortune makes an early morning visit to Tomioka Hachimangu Shrine in Monzen-naka-cho.
Bottom right Tour boats and tugboats make up most of the traffic on the Sumida River.
Below A young angler tries his luck in a Tsukijima Island canal.

Tsukiji

Right next to the Ginza, once thought of as the gate to high modernity, lies Tsukiji, still thought of as the last gasp of the low city. It still holds a number of plebeian markets, including the Tsukiji *shijo*, the largest wholesale fish market in the world, where early morning auctions are held, where wholesale dealers, nearly a thousand of them, operate their stalls. It is also prominent on the foreign tourists must-see list, though few Japanese visit it and the fish mongers themselves have complained

that the early morning foreigners are a great nuisance.

But Tsukiji has long been attracted to foreigners. The name itself means 'filled-in land,' and the territory was reclaimed as early as the 1700s. Mainly swampy marshlands, it was never popular with the inhabitants of the lower city. Therefore, when it was thought necessary to do something about the increasing number of foreigners in the country, it was agreed that they should all settle in unpopular Tsukiji, which opened to them in 1867.

It boasted a brand new hotel, the Hoterukan (200 rooms and a staff of 100), a hospital, and a handy red-light district, designed for the presumed needs of foreign gentlemen.

Despite such attractions, however, Tsukiji was no more popular with the new foreign tenants than it had been with its Japanese inhabitants. The problem was solved only by the great fire of 1872 that consumed hotel and brothels alike. From these ashes rose the

Above A skilled hand preps tuna for auction. **Left** A huge billboard tuna glows after sunset above one of the many seafood shops that surround the Tsukiji Fish Market.

Right Vendors select and bid on surprisingly expensive fresh tuna at the Tsukiji Fish Market, officially known as the Tokyo Metropolitan Central Wholesale Market.

Ginza, a major commercial center and long a symbol for modernity.

Marginalized Tsukiji became an area of small businesses—pottery, metal goods, tools—with St. Luke's Hospital, one of the best in the city, nearby, and that foreign-tourist mecca, the fish market, only a short distance away,

Now, however, progress threatens even that. Crowded piers, silted waterfronts and a general decrepitude have encouraged talk of a new fish market, this one further away from the city, out in the bay where it would be more accessible to fishing vessels, if not to foreign tourists.

Pages 64–65 The docks and busy display areas of the early morning fish market are filled with tuna and tuna buyers at dawn.

Nihonbashi

Down from Ueno, Akihabara and Kanda, and up from Ginza, Nihonbashi is named after the bridge that still distinguishes this old part of the capital.

The first bridge to span the narrow Nihonbashi River was built in 1603. Later replacements were repeatedly burned up in the many Edo fires, and the present bridge (the 20th, a Renaissance-style structure made of iron) was constructed in 1911.

This bridge was early its career deemed the center of the whole country (Nihonbashi literally means "Bridge of Japan") and a copper plate embedded in the center of the structure states that right here is the starting point of all of Japan's national roads. Conversely, highway signs all over the country still report the distance to Tokyo in terms of kilometers to Nihonbashi.

In 1999 the structure was designated an official "Cultural Asset," but the honor came too late. Affluence and ambition had decreed that the Bridge of Japan be obscured by the convenience of an overhead highway that considerably shadows whatever distinction the bridge itself may have had.

Indeed, the site may now be read as geological strata. At the bottom there is what is left of the canal that the structure bridges—now channelled, straightened, and forgotten. On its sunken shores are the stone ponts of the Edo-period bridge. On top of these is

the 1911 bridge, cast metal with ornamental unicorns and "Oriental" dogs (once emblems of a happy East/West symbiosis), and over it all roars the present century in the form of a packed elevated highway which just misses the heraldic beasts but renders the bridge itself almost invisible in the sense that no one notices it anymore.

The resulting triumph of convenience and affluence fits the atmosphere of Nihonbashi itself. Early, commerce moved in when the military aristocracy, finding the hills of the high city more salubrious, moved out. Here was first built the famous Nihonbashi fish market, now at Tsukiji; here the Bank of Japan erected its head office;

here were founded the department stores of Mitsubishi and Shirokiya. So great was the concentration of new money that, until recently, Nihonbashi was known as "the Wall Street of Japan." And what is an obscured bridge to this?

Above left A bronze dragon stands above the balustrade of Nihonbashi Bridge.
Above Jet skis zip underneath the historic Nihonbashi Bridge, while elevated expressways block the view overhead.
Right Gaudiesque design and good coffee attracts customers to the La Boheme Cafe in Kyobashi.

Left Two entrepreneurs sell handmade *mochi* ricecakes from their truck in front of a fashion boutique's summer sale, the latter heralded with Mt. Fuji and Hokusai waves.
Below A young woman in her work uniform walks by a construction site wall decorated with an old Edo-era woodblock print of citizens crossing Nihonbashi Bridge.
Right top An exotic welcome greets customers at Mitsukoshi Department Store's main entrance in Nihonbashi, with its guardian lion statues.
Right middle The owner of a traditional Japanese restaurant opens shutters decorated with a Hokusai woodblock print.
Right bottom The stone and glass facade of the Bank of Tokyo-Mitsubishi UFJ reflects the surrounding Nihonbashi business district.

Opposite The sunny atrium of the Mandarin Oriental Tokyo Hotel has a bamboo garden in its Italian restaurant at the Nihonbashi Mitsui Tower.
Left Morning sunlight illuminates the impressive stone facade and a vigilant security guard at the entrance to the Bank of Japan headquarters in the Nihonbashi district.
Right Sculptural ceiling lamps decorate the Oriental Lounge of the Mandarin Oriental Tokyo Hotel atop the Nihonbashi Mitsui Tower.
Below Newlyweds pose for photos in the spacious lobby of the Mandarin Oriental Tokyo Hotel.

Marunouchi

Marunouchi, the area around the west side of Tokyo Station, was originally an inlet of Edo Bay. With the castle going up virtually on its shores, it was not long before more space was needed, and the land was filled in, beginning in the late 16th century. On it the shogun's retainers, the *daimyo* from various parts of the country, built their mandatory mansions. Marunouchi (a name which means "within the circle," referring to the castle) originally held so many of these homes that the area became known as *daimyo koji* (daimyo alley.)

It was also an early home to various magistrates, among the most powerful being the finance magistrate. So it was fitting that, over the years, the Marunouchi district became the financial center of Edo. The three largest banks are still headquartered here, and it is here that big businesses strive for head offices. Here too things cost most: the phrase "Marunouchi price" refers to the frankly overpriced shops and restaurants now found in the many new buildings spotting the area.

It is here too that, since 1914, Tokyo Station debouches, making the place what has been called the "doorway to Tokyo." It remains the highest revenue-earning station in Japan, but it is not the largest—Shinjuku Station is now that, and both it and Ikebukuro Station handle more passengers.

Located to the north of Marunouchi,

Otemachi was named after the Ote gate of the Imperial palace, a structure still plainly visible. Here big business and banks also crowd, as well as the headquarters of three of the "big five" Tokyo newspapers.

As the new complex of Marunouchi/Otemachi stretches skyward, the views of the Imperial plaza and palace also grow. Originally there was some criticism that big business should not in any sense so overlook royalty. The combination of custom and convenience silenced such complaints, however, and for the first time those now dining in expensive ease in one of the top restaurants of a Marunouchi skyscraper can see more of the Imperial reserves than had ever before been visible to any of Japan's citizens.

Above A sleek new *Shinkansen* bullet train glides past the Tokyo International Forum and right through the middle of Yurakucho.
Right Gingko trees line Daimyokoji Avenue, crisscrossed with traffic and pedestrians, in the Marunouchi business district.

Above Businessmen wait for the light to turn green near Tokyo Station.

Below A traditional gardener climbs a tree without ropes or ladders for pre-spring pruning in the Marunouchi district.

Right A young couple relaxes on a sofa inside the soaring 60-meter high atrium of the Tokyo International Forum.

Opposite top A limousine driver waits in front of a mural during restoration work at Tokyo Station.

Opposite bottom Commuters flow with relative ease through Tokyo Station during the weekday morning rush.

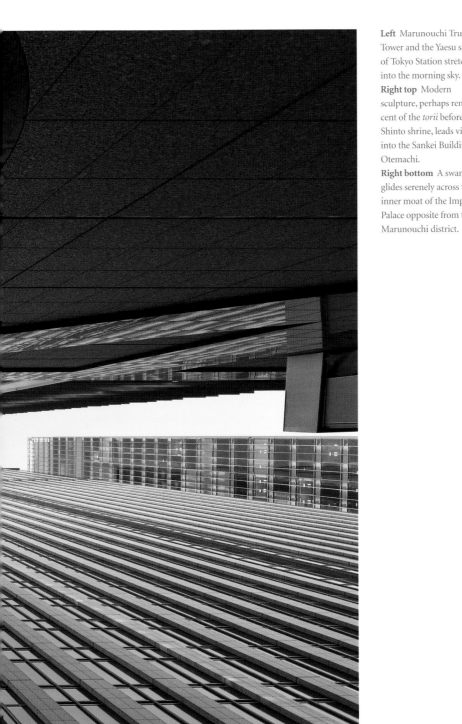

Left Marunouchi Trust Tower and the Yaesu side of Tokyo Station stretch into the morning sky.

Right top Modern sculpture, perhaps reminiscent of the *torii* before a Shinto shrine, leads visitors into the Sankei Building in Otemachi.

Right bottom A swan glides serenely across the inner moat of the Imperial Palace opposite from the Marunouchi district.

THE MID CITY

"Every city has its high points, but Tokyo is all exclamation points."

Above A fashionable young mother and daughter enjoy panoramic views of the
surrounding city from inside the Tokyo Tower Observatory.
Right A telephoto view reveals the observatory ringing the elegant steel girder
construction of Tokyo Tower.

THE MID CITY

What we will call mid-city was created through financial fiat. With the growing fissure between the waning military aristocracy and the waxing power of the townsfolk, something like an economic vacuum appeared. After the fall of the Tokugawa *bakufu*, after the consequent Meiji Restoration, it was the merchants who rushed in to fill it. They had the most money and so it was they who guided the fortunes of the growing city.

Since it was one of the beliefs of the Meiji period that the Western way was the modern way, the businesses of the low city percolated west, aiming at the lucrative high city. What

was needed, it was decided, was a more modern venue, wide, straight avenues, squared blocks of business. Would-be city planners spoke optimistically of something like Paris.

When it came to actually building what became mid-city Tokyo, however, it was found that the plots of land available were too small for such a grandiose scheme. The land on which Ginza, the first mid-city venue, is built is squared blocks of building, true, but these straight avenues soon peter out into the small lots of the familiar Tokyo tangle.

In any event, comparisons with Paris had to be shelved. Ginza at its widest is less than 30 meters across, nothing like the Champs-Elysées, which is 70. Even the Ginza sidewalks are only six meters wide, vast for Japan, but narrow compared to the nearly 12 meters of the Parisian boulevard.

In the years since then, the problem of small plots has become even more extreme. After developer Minoru Mori decided to build his Roppongi Hills complex, it took him 17 years to buy all the land necessary to its completion.

The first beginnings of the mid-city itself did not take that long, however, and one of the reasons is that there were already a number of businesses ready to move into the newly created spaces. These were there due to the ambitions of the various merchants of the low city.

Selling under the Tokugawa regime had been a much supervised affair, with each shop specializing: kimono, clogs, implements for the coiffeur, and so forth. There was a degree of

advertising, to be sure, actors promoting lines of dress and the like, but nothing like the present standard, where it is estimated that the average Tokyo consumer is subjected to 3,000 advertisements a day.

With the new freedom under the Meiji emperor, specialization was no longer enforced. Rather, there came the notion of freely selling everyone everything—a mercantile ideal. Among other novelties thus spawned was that Japanese institution, the *depato*.

Though the first of these department stores, Mitsukoshi, modeled its original building (destroyed in the 1923 earthquake) after the American Wanamaker department store, the uses of these emporia soon became "Japanese"—that is, they early began to sell culture and entertainment as well as merchandise.

Most contemporary department stores now have art galleries, as well as gadgets for the entire family. When the New York Museum of Modern Art was asked to lend canvases for Japan's first big postwar Monet show, it balked when told that the venue was a department store, and only agreed when it was convinced that this was the Japanese way.

MoMA probably had something like Macy's or Gimbel's in mind, but the Japanese department store is far different. It is, indeed, much like what used to be called in the West an emporium or, in piquant Japanese terminology, the nandemo-ya, the "we sell no matter what store."

Among the many commodities supplied by the department store—in addition to full lines of clothing, furniture, etc.—is an enormous selection of food. The largest is offered by the Tobu Department Store in Ikebukuro, where the "Food Hall" contains nearly 250 different vendors. To sweeten the sell, free mouth-sized samples are given out, and it has been maintained that, if you time yourself properly at the Shinjuku branch of Isetan Department Store, a full and free luncheon is possible.

The first two of Tokyo's department stores, Mitsukoshi and Shirokiya, were located at either end of the bridge at Nihonbashi and both were thus poised to slide into what became the Ginza shopping area of mid-town, then race up into the reaches of the high city itself.

In the resulting land rush, there was not only the difficulty of small plots but also very little city planning. Aside from the Ginza, which was designed to be grand, a real esplanade, there are in Tokyo very few vistas, long straight avenues. And just as

there are few vistas, so are there no promenades; just as there is no public display of stately buildings, so there is no place for stately walking about.

The grand sight of an entire avenue—one discovered by diarist John Evelyn in 1644 when he first saw Rome's Via Pia and proclaimed it "one of the most glorious sights for state and magnificence that any city can show a traveller"—is rarely found in Tokyo.

There is, to be sure, the Ginza avenue itself, but this throughfare was never intended as a civil promenade, it was intended as a commercial promenade. As such, it has been quite successful in that it has had many imitators. It is estimated that there are almost 500 "Ginzas" in the rest of Japan and that "Ginza" appears in the titles of over 50 pop tunes (while Mt. Fuji is mentioned in only a dozen or so). But while one strolls on the Ginza (*ginbura* it is called) one does not do so in any way that John Evelyn would recognize. One strolls in order to shop.

There are in Tokyo shorter stretches that might have aspired to the state of the promenade—the ginko-tree lined Aoyama entry to Meiji Park, the Omote-Sando "boulevard"—but these are not long enough to be a proper promenade and, in any event, are rarely used as such.

In fact, the only promenades to be found in Tokyo are those temporary ones more or less constructed by the citizens themselves and much criticized by the traffic authorities—the Sunday gatherings on the single stretch of straight street in Harajuku, various romping grounds in Akihabara, the Friday night routs at Roppongi Crossing.

Nor is there any real way get a representative view of Tokyo. In Paris one climbs up to Sacre-Coeur and there is the city, spread out, all avenues visible. In Rome one may choose among seven hills. Similar city views abound in Edinburgh, Budapest, San Francisco. In Tokyo, however, there are no heights from which to look down over the city as though upon a living map—though there are in Kobe, Nagasaki and Hakodate.

There was, until the age of the ubiquitous skyscraper, only one place from which such a vista was possible, someplace which had, indeed, been constructed with just this purpose in mind. This was mid-town's Tokyo Tower.

Modeled on Paris' Eiffel Tower, Tokyo's is not only higher (by 36 feet/13 meters) but lighter—it weight just 4,000 tons as compared to the 7,000 tons of the Paris edifice. Visited by nearly four million people annually, it has, since its inauguration in 1958, offered a view of Tokyo, and for decades remained the single vantage point.

And what does one see from the top of the tower? One sees just what the English poet Anthony Thwaite saw on his first helicopter ride over Tokyo in 1986: ". . . a dense sprawling huddle of smaller buildings, so closely jammed together than it is almost impossible to see the narrow streets that twist between them."

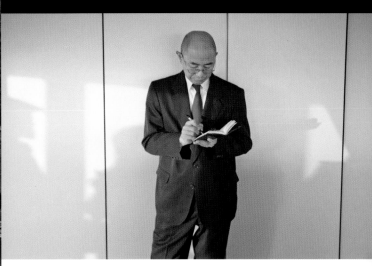

One pattern does emerge from the Tokyo Tower view, however. Just as Mark Girouard observed that an aerial view of Manhattan was really "a three-dimensional diagram of property values and rent levels," so the view of Tokyo from the top platform shows clusters of bigger buildings dwindling as the cheaper sections (the Bronxs or Brooklyns of Tokyo) are reached, though prices grow skyward near any mode of transportation no matter how far out. The resulting pattern indicates the worth of land in Tokyo, or at least its price, but it tells little of the scenes it creates, and avoids.

Tokyo, for example, is not beautiful and never tried to be. Beauty implies a certain balance, a kind of repose, a suggestion of timeless values and a kind of permanency in this

Above left to right A sculpture garden adds a classical European touch amidst recent reconstruction near Shiodome-Shimbashi (extreme left). Designer-brand fashion stores (here including Chanel, Cartier, Bvlgari, Louis Vuitton and De Beers Ginza), command the main corners in Ginza (second from left). The Yurikamome elevated train connects the Shidome business complex with the Odaiba district on Tokyo Bay (third from left). The newly replaced Naka-no-hashi Bridge crosses over the tidal seawater of Shioiri Pond, at the Nakajima Teahouse inside Hama-Rikyu Gardens (second from right). In warm afternoon sunlight, an attendant keeps track of things inside the Tokyo Tower Observatory (extreme right).
Bottom left Tea served inside Rikugien Garden reflects the season with a green- colored sweet in the spring.

impermanent world. Tokyo has none of this, just as it has no celebrated views or spots picturesque, and beauty itself depends upon just the kind of integration that Isabella Bird early accused the city of lacking. Architectural critic Peter Popham has noted that the reasons "for Tokyo's ugliness is this lack of integration." However, as he goes on to say, perhaps consequently, the integrative failure of many Western cities "has not touched Tokyo at all, as there is nothing to damage in this way."

A result is a certain lack of style—if one defines style as something typified by the unifications of, say, Bruges or Venice. All of the new Tokyo buildings are in simple, basic Big Business Moderne.

This lack of style is augmented by the fact that it is all done in Tokyo Impermanent. Even though the building materials are no longer wood and plaster and tile, but steel and stone and glass, Tokyo's rate of architectural erosion has not slowed.

Buildings are, due to the stern laws of economics, routinely destroyed to make room for others which will just as shortly be themselves knocked down.

The result is a singular cityscape. The effect is that of some national exposition several years after it has closed. There is the same urge to impress, to attract the eye for the moment, to sacrifice any idea of unity to the economic ends of diversity.

Now that the Tokyo view has been augmented by the newly built towers of Roppongi, Midtown, and Shiodome, Tokyo Tower itself will be augmented—by the New Tokyo Tower, a much taller structure now being contemplated, across the river, beyond even the reaches of the low city, where the land is still cheap enough. The land on which the present tower rests is now far too expensive to be wasted on a simple tourist attraction like this. Besides, it is right in the way of the planned pathway of a new set of skyscrapers.

Back in 1895, Lafcadio Hearn, best-known of Western authorities on the country, writing to his friend, Nishida Sentaro, stated that "there is no Japan like Tokyo." This prescient observation remains as true today (despite all the copies of the Ginza) as it was then. Although the provinces all attempt the Tokyo look, none succeed. The capitals of Japan's prefectures now look alike—there is architecturally no telling one from the other—since all were reconstructed at the same time after their WWII destruction.

They contain little of the extravagance of Tokyo. This is because they cannot afford it. Tokyo, after all, accounts for 40 percent of Japan's entire economy. Money flows into the capital but less regularly flows out. Even so, Tokyo's rate of development is so accelerated that there is always a money crunch somewhere. Asked how he could continue with his doubtless enormous debts to build wave after wave of skyscraper complexes, Developer Minoru Mori replied simply: "I cannot afford to quit."

The look of the city is the result of its truly burn-and-slash history of construction. The Tokyo way of making things is at every point—every point after cost, that is—to accommodate convenience, and such an attitude does not lend itself readily toward preservation.

At the same time, the gleaming high rise will often contain in its basements or along its plazas those neighborhood establishments (fruit stores, beauty shops, etc.) that it

Above left to right Office workers walk from Shiodome Station on their way to work in the Shiodome business complex (extreme left). Department store window displays are an ongoing exhibition in the underground passageways at Ginza Station (second from left). A Buddhist monk chants his way slowly through Ginza (third from left). Quiet and space, rare commodities in Tokyo, may be discovered inside Hama Rikyu Garden at the mouth of the Sumida River (third from right). A futuristic globe-shaped observatory sits atop the Fuji TV headquarters in the bayside Odaiba district (second from right). A young man proudly attired in Chanel queues on the sidewalk at the grand opening of the Ginza Chanel store (extreme right). **Opposite bottom** A Zen landscape fills the exhibition space at Maison Hermes in Ginza.

displaced in order to be built in the first place. A location in the new edifice was a condition for the land sale, and something like a continuation of the old neighborhood was an unintended result.

The human animal (particularly the genus *japonicus*) likes its burrow best and the stated aims and ambitions of the visionary town planner are often opposite this. Nonetheless (everywhere as well, but in Tokyo more visibly) the cells of the city crowd together to create a living, natural, organic hive, one especially suited to the people who live in it.

This is what many a Tokyo resident believes. One, Vivienne Sato, typical mid-towner, famous TV "talent," sometimes called "a unique cultural concierge," thinks so. She says that "Every city has its high points, but Tokyo is all exclamation points . . . It keeps getting better, even though it's already the best."

Ginza

A major mercantile complex, a long straight street, site of some of the more expensive stores, with large neighborhoods on either side (West Ginza, East Ginza), this famous area started late. Originally just a strip of land squeezed between the outer moats of the palace and the shores of the bay, it did not even begin to develop its own character until after the Tokyo fire of 1872 and the government's decree that the city be fireproofed.

Ginza therefore was to be built of brick, and a foreign architect was brought over to supervise this novel construction. Completed, the district held nearly 1,000 brick structures (as compared to the mere 20 or so in the rest of the city). Noted traveller Isabella Bird saw it in 1878 and said that it most resembled "the outskirts of Chicago."

In any event, these solid, sturdy, fireproof structures did not last. They had all been torn down even before WWII. One of the reasons was the rising price of Ginza land. A square foot of Ginza still costs much more than a square foot anywhere else, the reason for this being the space and style necessary for merchandising.

This—selling and buying—was always Ginza's main occupation. The main avenue running through the Ginza area, and now itself taking the name, has been called, in emulation of New York, "The Fifth Avenue of the Orient."

In terms of merchandising, the comparison is apt. Home of many of the major department stores, the place has more recently turned itself in a mall-like strip of designer buildings: Dior, Chanel, Hermes, Gucci, and many more each have their own proud edifices.

All this money fits Ginza's origins. It was originally the site of the Tokugawa silver mint (*gin-za*) and is now just as much Rodeo Drive as it is Fifth Avenue.

Here, over the decades, the well-off have shopped and wandered. They had their tea at the Shiseido Parlor, or went to the Fugetsudo coffee shop, or the Lion Beer Hall in its art-deco splendor—all of which places are, oddly, still there.

Left Chanel, Cartier and De Beers Ginza dominate this strategic corner in the heart of Ginza.
Right A lone visitor savors a contemplative moment inside the modern exhibition space at Maison Hermes in Ginza.

Above A woman in traditional kimono checks her mobile phone while strolling by the Chanel Store in Ginza.
Left Pedestrians enjoy a curious look at a Great Dane on Ginza's Chuo-dori (Central Avenue), closed to traffic on Sundays.

Right Window-display artists put finishing touches on a new creation at Chanel in Ginza.
Below The organically-shaped windows of the Mikimoto Ginza 2 Building create a new landmark in Ginza.

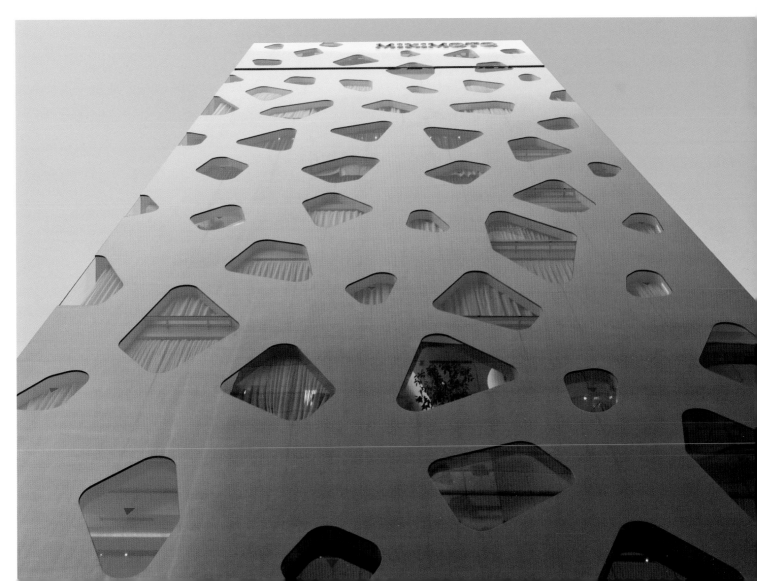

Above left A young man reclines in his gleaming red Ferrari while parked on Ginza's Central Avenue.

Above right A couple with a toddler pass by another Ginza baby.

Below A beauty queen highlights the Electrical Parade of the Grand Ginza Festival, held annually in mid-October.

Above left A Buddhist monk seeks alms from busy shoppers in Ginza.
Above right Pedestrians roam freely on a "Pedestrian Heaven" Sunday in Ginza.

Below A futuristic prototype electric commuter vehicle is introduced at the Nissan Auto Showroom in the center of Ginza.

Right A memorial at Nakabashi marks the birthplace of Kabuki in 1624 at the first Edo-era kabuki theater, Saruwaka-Nakamura-Za.

Hibiya

Next to the Imperial Plaza Hotel, west from Ginza, Hibiya Park might not be Tokyo's largest park (Ueno is), but it is among its earliest, having been opened to the public in 1903. Before that the land was all Imperial: a fragment of the castle escarpment still stands there, testifying right behind the Hibiya crossing police box.

What is now the park was originally the site of several of the *daimyo* mansions. With the Meiji Restoration of 1868, however, the *daimyo* permanently retired to their home provinces, and the 40-some acres they had occupied was in 1872 turned into a parade ground, Emperor Meiji keeping up the military tradition by reviewing the troops there.

As the land increased in value, however, a number of more lucrative plans were suggested. One was that these empty acres ought to contain a new bureaucratic center, and in 1886 a government planning office drew up such plans. Before these went too far, however, it was found that the land (all of it reclaimed—Hibiya was where the bay once lapped) could not support the weight of the buildings.

Something lighter being needed, a park was ordained—one that would perform the function of symbolizing the fusion of East and West, a Meji-era ambition. This desired state was to be reached by educating the public to cut off their top-knots, wear suits and

dresses rather than kimono, adopt to the Gregorian calendar, and eat beef.

This wish was reflected equally in the Rokkumeikan, an ornate East-West meeting place nearby, and then later in the Imperial Hotel, now just across the street.

Hibiya Park was thus designed to reflect a happy symbiosis. It has three sections in the Japanese style, two in the more formal Western, and its claims to international concerns include an enormous rock brought back all the way from Antarctica.

Locally, Hibiya Park offers shade and greenery and traditionally some privacy for dating couples. The police used to raid the place (the first such occurrence was in 1908 and the couples were fined), but since then the youngsters have

Above A *Shinkansen* bullet train rolls past the Yurakucho Mullion Building, crossing Daimyokoji Avenue and Harumi Avenue, and cutting right through the middle of Yurakucho.

Above right A bronze statue stands alone in a snowy Hibiya Park.
Right A modern sculpture constructed of bamboo, with references to traditional *ikebana* (flower arrangement), decorates the main lobby of the Peninsula Tokyo Hotel.

moved on to Shibuya and Shinjuku, and the police force—like the park itself—have mellowed considerably.

Left Spring is definitely in the air at Hibiya Park, where one businessman sings aloud beneath a flowering camellia, while another snaps photos in the background.
Below A spiral staircase leads down to a small Zen rock garden inside the Peninsula Tokyo Hotel

Above A cherry tree in full bloom softens the sleek architecture of Chanter Plaza in Yurakucho.
Below A bride is all smiles across from Hibiya Park.

Shimbashi

Unlike Ginza, Shimbashi, just to the south, did not modernize. Few brick buildings went up and it long continued as a small-time merchandising artisan district. Metaphorically, Ginza looked to the west, but Shimbashi continued to gaze east. Shimbashi even had a traditional geisha district—Yanagimachi—one that managed to last longer than any other in the city, although it has now entirely vanished.

Modernization, however, slowly invaded. Shimbashi Station, the terminus of Japan's first railway, the Tokaido Main Line, was inaugurated as early as 1872, the year of the great Tokyo fire that occasioned brick-town Ginza.

Many are the stories of east-west mismatches at Shimbashi Station. One such story tells of early travelers properly taking off their shoes in order to board the train and then being surprised at not finding them when they reached their destination.

A replica of the first Shimbashi station is now visible next door in Shiodome, surrounded by glass and steel and instructive texts, looking like the Meiji period embalmed.

With the completion of the Shiodome complex, however, the tussle between the east and west was over. West won.

Originally marshland (the name means "keeping out the tide"), Shiodome remained for years undeveloped, a humble freight yard adjacent to Shimbashi. In 1995, however, the Tokyo Metropolitan Government decided to make it a new urban center.

Shiodome is now a mass of skyscrapers, and has become what the city fathers call "a city within the city." It has also eclipsed the Shimbashi that spawned it, which now, like the frog in the well, languishes in this shadow of the future.

The new Shiodome houses the head offices of many leading corporations. The 50-storey Carett Building contains the offices of Dentsu, Japan's leading advertising agency, and the Nittelle

Tower, almost as high, is home to Nippon Television. Along with these are the boutiques, restaurants, spas, and hotels that invariably accompany corporate Japan.

Shimbashi, right next door, may have a MacDonald's or a Starbucks or two, but it feels shrunk and dowdy at the feet of such enterprise.

Above A giant skylight brightens the long passageway between the Conrad Tokyo Hotel and Shiodome Sumitomo.
Right Shiodome rises like a contemporary castle, high above surrounding buildings in Shimbashi.
Opposite A small vermilion-colored Shinto shrine is tucked underneath the NTV Tower in the Shiodome complex.

Right Wall-size advertisements line the walls of the Shiodome Concourse.
Below A patron is silhouetted behind a frosted glass window etched with calligraphy at a Chinese restaurant inside the Tokyo Shiodome Building.

Above A *sarariman* (office worker) passes through an old alleyway in Shimbashi.
Left The elevated Yurikamome Line passes through the new skyscrapers of Shiodome.

Right A businessman casts a shadow onto a commuter train pulling into Shimbashi Station.

Odaiba

Here a slice of the future is laid next door to the Low City—right in the middle of Tokyo Bay. It is a vast parcel of reclaimed land anchored to the six island-fortresses constructed in 1853 by the Tokugawa shogun to protect Edo from Commodore Matthew Perry's armed fleet, which had menacingly arrived in the bay the same year.

As early as 1959 there was a plan to fill in Tokyo Bay and make space for an artificial city to be called Neo-Tokyo. The most remarkable of the many planned architectural wonders was a four-kilometer-high, cone-shaped skyscraper that would have been taller than Mt. Fuji.

Nothing came of such plans except a major loss of funding. Finally re-zoned in 1995, the new, much more modest island of Odaiba called itself Tokyo Teleport Town and decided to become "a showcase for futuristic living." After a number of further financial tribulations, hotels, companies, and shopping malls began moving to the artificial island.

In addition to the futuristic headquarters of Fuji Television, there is the Aqua City shopping center, the 225-meter Palette Town Ferris Wheel, the Big Sight exhibition center, and Tokyo Leisure Land, a 24-hour video-gaming, karaoke, and bowling center. There is also the Venus Fort shopping mall, its name a graceful reference to

the six island-fortresses that so conspicuously failed to keep out the Western invaders. There is also a miniaturized Statue of Liberty now welcoming those once barred.

Odaiba's skyline rivals that of Shanghai in its bright lights and improbable modernism. One gets there by riding the Yurikamome New Transit Monorail, fully automated, no driver; one admires the laser-lit television head office; one examines the Toyota Mega Web, a giant car showroom; one rides the Wheel, a complete revolution taking sixteen minutes.

But the most enticing spectacle has little to do with Tokyo Teleport Town. It is the view of the rest of Tokyo as seen from the waters of Odaiba. Megacity Tokyo soars, a fantastic view capped by the towers of Shinjuku—all to be seen from the center of the old town itself—Tokyo Bay.

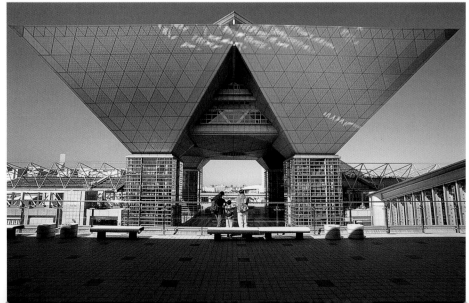

Left The relatively wide-open spaces of Odaiba encourage creative architecture like the Tokyo Big Sight International Exhibition Center.

Above Rainbow Bridge crosses shipping lanes and old defensive islands (constructed in 1853) beyond the Hotel Nikko Tokyo in the Odaiba district of Tokyo Bay.

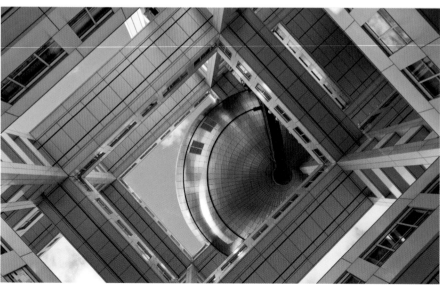

Above The observatory atop Fuji TV headquarters in Odaiba looks out across Tokyo Bay and Rainbow Bridge to the sprawling mass of Tokyo Megacity.
Left A look skyward reveals the complex architectural structure leading up to the globe-shaped observatory of Fuji TV headquarters.

Right top The fully-automated Yurikamome Elevated Railway glides past behind a fluttering Japanese National Flag.
Right Newlyweds exit stage left at the wedding chapel at the Hotel Nikko Tokyo in Odaiba.

Opposite top *Yakatabune* excursion houseboats add their lanterns to the colorful reflections filling Tokyo Bay.
Opposite bottom left The expanses of Odaiba's Center Promenade host temporary exhibition spaces like the Nomadic Museum, created with shipping containers and paper tubes by architect Shigeru Ban.
Opposite bottom right The Odaiba boardwalk is perfect for puppy-walking.
Above Ariake Sports Center, the Teleport Bridge, and elevated expressways create a Blade Runner landscape at twilight.
Right Windsurfers skim across the bay at Odaiba Seaside Park.

Shinagawa

When Tokyo was still Edo, it was fringed by post-stations on each of the major roads leading in and out. These were known as the "five mouths" of the city. Among these, Shinagawa was the busiest. It led south, and was the first of the 53 stages of the *Tokaido,* the main coastal road to the Kyoto, a route famous for inspiring the Hokusai and Hiroshige woodblock series.

It was also one of the largest post-stations, second only to the Yoshiwara, the northern entrance, the one with a welcoming licensed quarter that flourished until fairly recently (1957). Post-stations, where the traveler rested before entering or leaving Edo, were famous for such amenities. Shinagawa had a flourishing red-light quarter as well.

It does so no longer. The past is over and the present is here. Now Shinagawa contains the most embassies and claims the highest concentration of hotels in the city; it is also said to contain more skyscrapers than anywhere in Tokyo but Otemachi and Shinjuku.

This is the result of its having recently become the swiftest growing business-district in the capital. Originally the place lagged behind such fast-starters as Shinjuku, but the combination of becoming a major rail center and offering, for a time, affordable land prices, invited in many a new Shinagawa investor.

Mighty companies now have major branches and even central headquarters in this once isolated post town, among them Japan Air Lines, Canon, Sony, Panasonic and NTT Docomo. The west side of the station (known as Takanawa) has become a very upmarket residential area indeed, and the east side contains the handy (and manditory) Tokyo Regional Immigration Bureau, a place with which perforce most foreign residents are quite familiar.

Tokyo is, of course, famous for its swift urban metamorphosis, but the rate of change in Shinagawa has been unusual. You can still perhaps see old-fashioned houseboats backed by high-rise residences. Perhaps, but not for long. The busiest of the old post-stations of the past has become the portal into the future.

Above A sleek new *Shinkansen* bullet train slides into Shinagawa Station.
Above right With a *Shinkansen* rushing by in the background, a boat captain carefully steers his *yakatabune* excursion houseboat past others moored in a narrow canal just off the Sumida River.
Right A meticulously managed food kiosk is part of the new Shinagawa Station complex.

Above Morning
commuters swarm through
a connecting passage inside
Shinagawa Station.

Below A group of visitors
admire the spacious
courtyard garden at the
Shinagawa Station complex.

Above A mother leads her young daughters and their shadows into the sunlight at Shinagawa Station.
Right The upper level Starbucks makes a pleasant spot for a business break inside the station.

Hamarikyu

Located near the mouth of the Sumida River, south of Shimbashi and Shiodome, the Hamarikyu Onshi Teien, the last of the old Imperial parks, remains much as it always has been. Originally the shogun's hunting grounds, it until recently contained several duck ponds, and exhibitions of falconry are still occasionally held.

After more land had been reclaimed in 1654, the Hama Palace, an Imperial villa, was constructed. It provided accommodation for visiting local lords and, after 1871, when the Imperial family took possession, a roof over the heads of distinguished visiting foreigners.

One such was General Ulysses S. Grant, who spent several summer months there in 1879. He chatted with the young Emperor Meiji, complimented the chef on the excellence of his American-style fried potatoes, and fished in the lake, boated about by footmen.

Though the palace itself was dismantled in 1899, the gardens were still utilized for royal receptions until 1916, and are still used by the city for various civic celebrations.

All the building were destroyed, however, in the fire raids of 1945. The Japanese army had dug the gardens up to make antiaircraft emplacements, and the place had become a military target. Even after WWII was over, military associations continued. Though is was opened as a public park in the spring of 1946, the Allied Occupation Forces still had its uses for it—Allied garden parties and the like.

In 1952, however, after the end of the Occupation, the Hamarikyu Teian was appointed a "Special Place of Scenic Beauty" and protected by the Cultural Properties Protection Law of Japan. This is why the garden—the tea-house, various gazebos reconstructed—does not appear too much changed and, in teeming mega-Tokyo, still appears pleasantly restful.

Though it has, after a fashion, remained, the surroundings have changed beyond all recognition. The gardens are now backed by the skyscrapers of Shiodome and elsewhere. A recent guidebook speaks of this, saying that the "the contrast between the old and the new is superb," but this impression depends entirely upon what you mean by superb.

With an ornamental pine tree in the foreground and the Shiodome business complex in the background, the refined Nakajima Teahouse reflects in the tidal water of Shioiri Pond at Hama-Rikyu.

Above Boats cruise up the
Sumida River alongside
Hamarikyu Gardens.
Left Yachts are anchored
in a sheltered canal
bordering the gardens.
Right A traditional paper
lantern glows warmly after
sundown inside
Hamarikyu Gardens.

Right Kimono-clad visitors admire the fresh Spring foliage and cherry blossoms inside Hamarikyu Gardens.
Below The Shiodome business complex forms a solid wall of light behind Hamarikyu Gardens and the Nakajima Teahouse casts sparkling reflections on the tidal seawater of Shioiri Pond. It perhaps functions as a contemporary borrowed landscape—a tradition in Japanese garden design incorporating distant scenery.

Rikugien

Early foreign travelers sometimes wrote home praising the greenery of Tokyo—but they were often comparing the new capital to Osaka, a city still notable for its lack of greenery. Actually, Tokyo does not rate very high in any list of the world's most park-filled cities. But those it does have are often memorable.

Take the Rikugien, for example, 25 acres in the middle of Tokyo still in its more or less its original state, as it was when built by the landscape architect Yanagisawa Yoshiyasu for the Shogun Tokugawa Tsunayoshi in 1702. It was donated to the city in 1938 and finally designated an Important Cultural Asset in 1953.

Its name, Rikugien, might be translated as "Six-Poem Garden," in reference to the six elements found in classical Japanese poetry. These are illustrated in the 88 "scenes" from famous poems.

Built around a pond, the garden is experienced as one strolls around it, clockwise, and the scenes are revealed. The most famous is the Togetsukyo Bridge, two large stone slabs laid parallel to each other and said to somehow refer to a famous poem about the moon moving in its own course as a crane calls from a nearby paddy.

Such oblique references (discernible only to cultured poetry readers) are typical of many Edo gardens, which often contain famous scenes from somewhere else: a bridge in Kyoto, for example, or a lake in China, or mythical Mount Sumeru—a large vertical stone standing on one end.

We are more familiar with such augmentation in Disneyland, which specializes in replicas of this kind, as seen in its various "lands," and attractions such as "It's a Small World." But Japan perhaps had the idea first.

Tokyo Disneyland is the most successful theme park ever contrived, and it obviously appeals to a culture where there is a whole aesthetic vocabulary that validates such borrowings as the "recollections" (*hikiuta*), and such representations (*hommondori*) of Japanese gardening. These stud many an Edo garden, where we cross a Kyoto bridge to reach a famous Chinese mountain, just as Splash Mountain leads to Space Mountain.

Above A bridge and a stone lantern are traditional elements of Japanese garden design.

Right Green tea and a seasonal sweet are served on a laquerware tray at the Fukiage Teahouse.

Opposite A *komomaki* (protective straw covering) is artfully wrapped around a 300-year-old *akamatsu* (red pine tree.)

Left A view straight up reveals the intricate construction of bamboo, reeds, rope and beautiful naturally-twisted tree limbs in the roof of Tsutsuji-no-chaya (Azalea Teahouse), which survives from the Meiji Period .

Left A boathouse and carefully-tended Japanese pine trees line the pond.

Above The branches of maple trees in fall hues hang over Togetsukyo Bridge, which is a simple construction of two huge stone slabs.

Below Bright red autumn leaves accent the shapely limbs of a Japanese maple.

THE HIGH CITY

A few days in Tokyo makes one wonder if
any more sheerly entertaining city ever existed.

Above The towers of the High City at dusk resemble modern castles.
Right The main entrance to Midtown Tokyo is a spacious public plaza with
sculpture and bamboo amidst a glass-and-steel canyon.

Yamanote, the High City, was originally conceived as a residential suburb. You did your business at the castle and then went home. The rest of Edo, to which you rarely went, was just Shitamachi, the low city. So, if you ranked high enough, the low lands were rarely visited. It was in the more salubrious hills that you lived. It was a good address, and it still is.

This is because in Tokyo, as in Edo before it, status is everything, though the status standard changes. There is said to be no more aristocracy, Japan is nominally a democracy, and the current samurai are the local captains of industry.

The new standard—prowess in buying and selling—is not all that recent however. An early traveller, Isabella Bird, noted that the highest creed consists of "bald materialism—material good its goal."

A later traveller, Stephen Mansfield, describes the phenomenon as it is now. "The visitor immediately understands why Tokyo is often described as the warehouse of the world. Advertising its production in innovative eye-catching ways, its buildings are covered with running commercial text and scroll, forests of signage . . . even the barriers surrounding construction sites aspire to a near commercial art form. Tall, freshly spray-painted and glossy, they are just as likely to be advertising images of construction models as they are to be publicizing chic brands . . ."

The plethora of publicity in the high city (less in the Low because of fewer potential buyers) often reaches the heights of pure decor. And, like a stage set, it is exciting to look at. At the same time, one must remember G.K. Chesterton's sage words (about New York's Broadway but fitting even better contemporary Tokyo): "What a glorious garden of wonder this would be for anyone who was lucky enough to be unable to read."

The splendid freedom of illiteracy informs (or disarms) the architecture of the place as well. Nothing any longer means what you, the foreign observer, have long thought it did. There is indeed a real freedom in finding that Doric columns do not mean a bank, nor red roof-tiles, Spain. Tokyo Station would look at home in Amsterdam but need not speak the same language; the Akasaka Detached Palace would fit nicely into Vienna but its imperial accent is entirely different; the towering high-rise of Tokyo City Hall in Shinjuku may speak in the patois of Dallas-Fort Worth but it is not saying the same thing.

Now with all this post-mod swarming, Babylonian, Baroque and Bel-Air Moderne all grouped incongruously together, one may more fully appreciate Isabella Bird's early aperçu: "It is singular that the Japanese, who rarely commit a solescism in their own architecture, seem to be perfectly destitute of perception when they borrow ours."

Such promiscuous clusterings come naturally to a culture that does not know what the original alluded to and does not care—we all use each others' idioms to suit our own meanings and we are rarely troubled by having to observe the integrity of any original.

After viewing the architectural excesses of mid- and high-cities, one wonders, in the midst of this architectural mélange, at Japan's reputation for social conformity. Also Japan's purported sense of a single style. Any style is mutable and over time changes shape. Just decades ago Japan was seen as the home of quiet good taste, of *shibui*, of *satori* and other Zen enlightenments. Now it is the home of manga and anime, the tenement of Pokémon, the den of Hello Kitty.

At the same time, there is a real connection between then and now. Just as Tokyo is Edo writ large, so all the baroque flourishes of Shibuya or Harajuku can be traced back to what used to be called "modern," the generic blank-box style (think Bauhaus) that originally came from Japan. Architect Richard Rogers, the man liable for Paris' Centre Pompidou, has said that the whole modern movement came from architects "looking at things like the Katsura Detached Palace" in Kyoto. The poet Henri Michaux, in Tokyo in 1932, noted that "the Japanese have been modern for ten centuries . . . Tokyo is a hundred times more modern than Paris." It still is and this all began with Edo. Perhaps that is one of the things that make it so livable. It fits our contemporary needs.

Let us take drinking, for example. Edo was already notably bibulous. When Richard Hakluyt went, circa 1565, he observed that the inhabitants "feed moderately but they drink largely." A later visitor, Truman Capote, called Tokyo "a barfly's Valhalla."

Indeed, there are over 40,000 bars in Tokyo. They come in all types and sizes, from the elegant watering holes of Ginza and the glittering supper clubs of Akasaka, to the cubbyholes of neon-drenched Shinjuku—the largest entertainment area in Tokyo, perhaps in all of Asia, perhaps in all of the world.

High town's Shinjuku has been called "a blinding maze of streets holding thousands of places, most of them friendly, all of them noisy: workmen's bars with saké and grilled squid; white collar bars with whiskey highballs and karaoke; hostess bars for company executives with scotch, smoked salmon, and no price lists anywhere."

Food also ensures livability and it is said you must search really hard in Tokyo to find a bad meal. Rather, good meals

Above left to right
Pedestrians hurry past the Big Hat entrance hall at Roppongi Hills (far left). An abstract sculpture marks the main plaza entrance to Midtown Tokyo (second from left). An impressive selection of sushi is illustrated outside a restaurant at Roppongi Crossing (third from right). A young woman in a *yukata* (summer kimono) consults her cellphone while casually leaning against a wall-size Chanel advertisement at Takashimaya Times Square department store in Shinjuku (second from right). Graphic shadows emphasize the architectural design elements of the Park Bridge passage leading from Midtown Plaza to Hinokicho Park at Midtown Tokyo (far right).

abound, though you pay for what you get. For those who do not want to pay too much, there are well over 20,000 ramen noodle restaurants in the capital, at which the average consumer consumes 43 servings a year.

For the satisfaction of other needs and greater livability, there are in Japan around 40,000 "love hotels," places where a "short time" (two hours) residence is encouraged. There are more such hotels in the country than there are 7-Eleven, Lawson, Family Mart and Circle K-Sunkus convenience stores put together. Tokyo's Shinjuku, like Asakusa's Yoshiwara before it, is a capital of the flesh, and Edo's sound economic stance toward pleasure is still strongly upheld.

In fact, in terms of sheer living, a few days in Tokyo makes one wonder if any more sheerly entertaining city ever existed. There is so much to do every day, and the opportunities seem to double after dark. Tokyo's high city is all proper addresses and high-priced residences. Yet, at the same time it is frenetic, feckless, in love with novelty, and equipped with wall-to-wall entertainment. The scope is vast and the choice enormous.

THE HIGH CITY

Tokyo's Shinjuku is packed, noisy, and never goes to sleep. One could wander all night enjoying all sorts of freedom, including a respite from architectural regimentation. Instead, a medieval Japanese castle contains a popular noodle eaterie; a plastic Tudor palace holds a coffee shop and in the dungeon is a "mammoth" bar; the Fontana di Trevi (in white plastic but with real water) serves as a pachinko parlor façade.

This creative mishmash of foreign styles, this international cornucopia, allows the critical foreigner room to carp. Henry Norman heard a diplomat say that "Japan, you see, is a bad translation." And Lincoln Steffins came, gazed about, and wrote: "Sometimes it looks as if Japan were created as a satire on Western civilization."

The implication is that modern Japan is in bad taste. Without our enquiring too closely into the foundations of that agreement known as good taste, one can affirm that a known brand of bad taste clearly proliferates—this is the sort known in the West as kitsch.

Indeed, Japan is the kingdom of kitsch, and Tokyo is it kapital. Food in restaurant windows, much more appetizing than the real food, is made of plastic; Mount Fuji ends up as a miniature tissue dispenser, the smoke from the volcano being the Kleenex. Kitsch (derived from the German *kitschen*) indicates cheapening, its attributes invariably including an adaptation from one medium to another: wallpaper imitating wood, or marble, or brick; the love hotel built to resemble Buckingham Palace. Kitsch at the same time always represents an effort to diminish scale and reduce function to merely domestic terms—in this case, Japanese ones.

But to cheapen also means to make more economical, and making small, making standard, indeed, making in the traditional Japanese manner involves a number of these attributes. There were and are standards, but these are for things Japanese and not for things foreign.

As the early traveler Percival Lowell recognized, "the Japanese have been a nation of importers, not only of merchandise, but also of ideas." And in its importing of attitudes, Japan was in the forefront in its early appreciation of foreign kitsch.

Also, now, traditional taste, no longer intelligible to the young, has been crafted into something new. These dead canons are the basis of the "Japanesque," itself a newer subspecies of kitsch. Polyester summer kimono with a clip-on *obi* belt; holy sutras gold-printed on neckties; discos entered through a chrome torii gateway; department stores with a holograph image of Jizo, popular Buddhist patron.

The confusion of styles that is typical kitsch ensures that one nullifies the other. The results are like a pousse-cafe, a rainbow drink of noted tastlessness, one with no single flavor, unless this consists of no flavor at all. Walking in a smart high-city neighborhood is like wading in a box of *wagashi*, traditional Japanese sweets, where each piece looks different and everything tastes the same.

At the same time, notice the exhilaration of this walk through the high town kapital of kitsch. Just as manga and anime have only one aim, to make us happy, so—as the great lesson of Pop Art the world over teaches us—there is freedom in the plainly popular, there is liberation in kitsch, there is consolation in frivolity.

In modern Tokyo as in old Edo, this playful spirit of *matsuri*

Above left to right Tokyo's Hard Rock Cafe, with its neon guitar and wall-climbing King Kong, is a popular Roppongi destination for foreign visitors (extreme left). Spiral staircases with illuminated steps ascend from the lobby at the Grand Hyatt Hotel in Roppongi Hills (second from left). Midtown Tower, the tallest building in Tokyo Prefecture, soars into a blue sky at the main entrance to Tokyo Midtown (third from left). Young women with cellphones attached create a trendy tableau with Louis Vuitton at Roppongi Hills (second from right). The giant poster of a pop singer wears an architectural hat at Dogenzaka crossing in Shibuya (extreme right).
Below left A morning rush of workers and commuter trains crosses Yasukuni Avenue with building-size posters as backdrop near Shinjuku Station.

is both an attraction and a necessity. Just under the frowning castle wall was the carnival plaza and the eating, drinking, dressed-up, dancing throng. Now, just under the sober, serious high-rise company headquarters is the saturnalian street, people still eating and drinking, still dressed up and dancing, all experiencing the consolations of pleasure.

Without the draconian stringency of the Edo *bakufu*, the license of the licensed quarters would perhaps not have been necessary, and without the rigors of the office workplace, the unpaid overtime, the need for the release of the bar and the brothel, the happy aural kinship of karaoke, and the oblivion of the pachinko parlor would not be so welcome, and the frenetic energy of people trying so hard to have a good time would not be so apparent.

But maybe this is what "livable" connotes, the opportunity to celebrate, to compensate. The recreational heights of the high city may resemble the over-populated excesses of *Blade Runner*, but these are malign in the film. Now, imagine all this wonderful and playful excess turned benign and you have livable Tokyo.

Roppongi

Like Hibiya, Roppongi began as a military center. The empty fields offered places for marching and drilling, and two wars (the Sino-Japanese War of 1894-95, and the Russo-Japanese War of 1905) required the exercise.

Roppongi's military associations continued even after the Japanese army was disbanded following its WWII defeat. The U.S. Army moved into the recently abandoned barracks.

With soldiers, however, come their special needs, and these include bars and "hostesses." Roppongi shortly again became a camp town, with the difference that the soldiers this time were not Japanese.

Since the soldiers were foreign, Roppongi itself grew into something like a foreign town, attracting a foreign population and those Japanese drawn by a perceived exotic life style. Clubs, discos, singles-bars, all of the impedimenta of foreign nightlife were to be found there, as well as prostitution, a nascent drug culture, and a decided *yakuza* influence.

As the price of land continued to rise, however, such businesses as these could not afford the further financial opportunities. Roppongi was, rather, seized upon by the wealthy waiting conglomerates, and the district again changed into something else.

Among the first of the resulting high-rise complexes was Roppongi Hills, a mega-complex, another "city within the city," completed in 2003 with apartments, shops, restaurants, theaters, and lots of office space, all resting on man-made hills that make the high city even higher.

Yet further high-rise complexes have now sprung up. Only half a mile away and several years later (2007) another was hatched, Mitsui-Fudosan's Tokyo Midtown. It is located on grounds formerly held by the Japan's de facto army, the Self Defence Force, and it too has a museum and lots of shopping space, as well as an even taller tower.

A third such Mori complex will extend itself from Akasaka down to Toranomon, and doubtless others are on the drawing boards. The predictable result will be whole rows of castles that dominate high-city Tokyo as did old Edo Castle before it burned down.

The observatory atop Mori Tower in Roppongi Hills offers a 360-degree view of Tokyo, as well as an art museum, shops and cafes.

Opposite top Roppongi Hills is one of many new contemporary "castles" in Tokyo Megacity.
Opposite bottom left A giant spider sculpture staretches above the plaza below Mori Tower.

Opposite bottom right A jogger is dwarfed by a large abstract sculpture in Midtown Garden.
Above Architect Kisho Kurokawa designed the undulating curves of the National Art Center.

Below left The Art Café atop the Mori Tower observatory in Roppongi is a quiet getaway with a marvelous view.
Below right Abstract marble sculpture, a circular skylight, and support

columns of symbolic "bamboo" brighten the underground passage connecting Midtown Tokyo and the Roppongi Metro Station.

Extreme left Three graces in *yukata* (summer kimono) stroll near Roppongi Hills.

Second left A spacious plaza is the main entrance to Midtown Tokyo.

Third left Two Lamborginis—one to drive, one an architectural accent—only in Roppongi.

Near left Cafes are located atop soaring concrete towers inside the impressive atrium of the National Art Center.

Opposite bottom The Japanese garden inside Hinokicho Park at Midtown Tokyo is a perfect spot to relax . . . or to use that ubiquitous cellphone.

Right A chrysanthemum-shaped stone basin collects maple leaves in the garden of a Roppongi residence.

Below Early springtime brings pink-and-white cherry blossoms and fresh greenery to the traditional garden at the International House of Japan.

Aoyama

The name of this affluent district, Aoyama (Blue Mountains), might be thought to refer to the hills of the high city, but in reality it was named after one Aoyama Tadanori, an officer who worked closely with the Shogun Tokugawa Ieyasu, and was given the area to build samurai mansions on. This he did and the land left over eventually became the Aoyama Cemetary.

Like most of the former inhabitants, however, he was wealthy, and this quality fits well into the contemporary Aoyama scene. The place, once open fields dotted with temples, shrines, and samurai mansions, has become one of the prime places for fashion houses, fine dining, and high-end shopping.

It was early called "a haven for youth" and, though the youngsters have now moved to the trendier locations of Harajuku and Shibuya, enough shoppers remain to fill the stores in what has become increasingly an up-market shopping mall.

Here are found not only the flagship buildings of name designers, such as the attention-getting Prada headquarters, but also the smaller houses of aspiring local brands such as Diesel Denim and Hysteric Glamour. Streets have been widened to accomodate expected traffic and Aoyama is well on its way to becoming the new Ginza.

It is very lively. It is also, in a sense, very dead, since Aoyama is the site of

Above Even a view straight up captures a cluster of Designer Brand boutiques, including Cartier and Omega, at Minami-Aoyama Square, with Prada just next door.

Right Pleasent multi-tasking on Aoyama Avenue—window shopping, dog walking and quality time with a friend.

one of the city's major cemeteries, one covering an area as large as does Paris's Pere Lachaise or London's Highgate. Among the illustrious inhabitants are Inukai Tsuyoshi, the assassinated prime minister, and writers Shiga Naoya and Mishima Yukio.

Established in 1872, long before fashion swept the area, the cemetery is also (along with Ueno Park and the Yanaka Cemetary) one of the best places to view the late March *sakura* (Japanese cherry) blossoms. Also one of the few, since many High Town places have lost their *sakura*. The trees were cut down long ago because the blossoms were thought too associated with the then *declassée* samurai.

If you were dead, however, it did not matter. The Aoyama Cemetary now annually fills up with cherry-blossom-viewing families. So much so that the avenues leading in have been widened. These widened streets now contain five times the number of vehicles they had before the widening, since more road also means more cars.

Salon
de
Garconne

Salon
de
Garconne

Tel
3404-0095

Open
10:00~19:30

TULB
TONE UP A LITTLE BIT

TULB

SALE SALE

Above A stylish young
lady zips across Aoyama
Avenue on her scooter.
Right A stylish older lady
strolls past Prada.

Above Prada at twilight is
a beautiful architectural/
fashion experience.
Right A young Japanese
restaurant worker in
Aoyama delivers hot (and
carefully balanced) meals
on his bicycle.
Far right A young man
successfully pulls off a
classic scarf-with-beret
look on Aoyama Avenue.

Akasaka

Located south of both the Imperial palace and the home of Japan's government, the National Diet Building, Akasaka has been called "Japan's corridor of power," and has long been associated with political puissance.

The district originally had great tracts of Imperial land and, as Edward Seidensticker wrote: "Had one been good at scaling walls and evading guards, one could have walked the whole way across the ward, from the city limits to the outer moat, without setting foot on private, non-royal land."

It eventually held parade grounds and palaces as well. During the Meiji era, low-city Kanda may have been among the wards holding the most people, and Nihonbashi may have had the highest population density, but Akasaka was home to both powerful aristocracy and government officialdom.

It was here that the Togu Palace was completed in 1908. Now known as the Akasaka Detached Palace, it remains a structure exceptionally lavish in that it was inspired by both Buckingham Palace and Versailles. It is presently the Imperial guesthouse. In it are lodged visiting kings, queens, popes, and other visitors of import.

Just up the street from Kasumigaseki, Japan's "Capitol Hill," Akasaka is also a place of more or less prestigious entertainment. It still has remnants of a once prosperous geisha district, and there are a number of expensive *ryotei*, Japanese-style restaurants. It was here that government officials once entertained each other, using their famously scandalous expense accounts. Now, though plebeian Korean barbecue eateries elbow the name sushi shops, the bureaucrats still assemble nightly.

Amid all this, signs of the past are few. One still visible is the Hie Shrine, dating back to 1478 but reconstructed as late as 1967, and the site of one of the rare high-city festivals, the *Sanno Matsuri* (June 15), once one of the three great festivals of Edo.

But Akasaka is not about the past. In his 1972 film, *Solaris*, the Russian director Andrei Tarkovsky found here his City of the Future. Here are the

Above An elaborate iron gate protects the main entrance to the Geihinkan, the Akasaka Detached Palace officially known as the State Guesthouse.
Above right Young newlyweds have their picture taken in the traditional Edo-era Japanese garden, once a samurai lord's residence, located inside the New Otani Hotel.
Below right New Year's worshippers may pass through a special circular *shimenawa* (sacred straw rope) for extra purification inside the central courtyard at Hie Shrine.

massive office buildings, the elevated highways criss-crossing the view, the crowded streets of things to come, all here, right now.

Opposite top A young couple pause to enjoy the view from an arched bridge in the traditional Edo-era Japanese garden at the New Otani Hotel.

Opposite bottom Cherry blossoms flutter past a *torii* gate at Hie Shrine.

Above A peek through a round window in central Akasaka finds chefs at work inside a seafood restaurant.

Right Dawn's first sunrays highlight architectural and fine masonry details—as well as serious police security—at the distinctive granite tower dome of the National Diet Building (completed in 1936), with the House of Representatives Office Building in the background.

Yoyogi

While the low city was settling into the patterns we can still observe, the high city was enlarging in a random fashion, driven by available land and how much it cost. One early section of the city contained only the fields and meadows of what is now Yoyogi.

Once site of some samurai mansions, these fields later became the scene of Japan's first powered airplane flight, accomplished in 1910. Later, the area became, like Hibiya and Roppongi before it, an army parade ground. After the war, military associations continued as it turned into Washington Heights, a residential area for U.S. Army officers.

Later, again big, wide and empty, the military meadows were selected as site for the 1964 Summer Olympics. This brought up the price of land and created Yoyogi as it is now. One single iconic building remains, the National Gymnasium, which was designed by the architect Tange Kenzo.

Yoyogi remains equally well known, however, as the original site of very low-city-like exhibitions of spontaneous streetlife. These still occur sporadically along the main Yoyogi avenue and on the short bridge between Harajuku Station and Meiji Shrine, and feature music, dancing, fashion, and other public preoccupations of the young.

The area is particularly associated with the harmless exhibition of *kosupurai* ("costume play"), which means youngish girls dressing up in costumes based on TV shows, pop bands, J-pop music, anime, and manga.

Such exhibitions (along with rockers, punks, bikers, etc.) have been dubbed dissident, and so interpreted by the local authorities who still ban them from time to time. The revelers then move to Akihabara, or outside Tokyo Dome in Suidobashi, though in actuality they are probably only rebelling against the boredom of peace and prosperity.

Despite the former vigilance of a military government and the present wariness of a paternalistic one, there have been many such spontaneous popular outbreaks in Japanese history—including a number of "peasant rebellions" and the famous *Eijanaika* ("Anything's ok") dancing craze of the late 1860s, where people-power was said to have threatened civic authority.

By comparison, anti-authoritarian Sunday exhibitions in Yoyogi and Harajuku are not to be taken seriously, though occasionally the police do so.

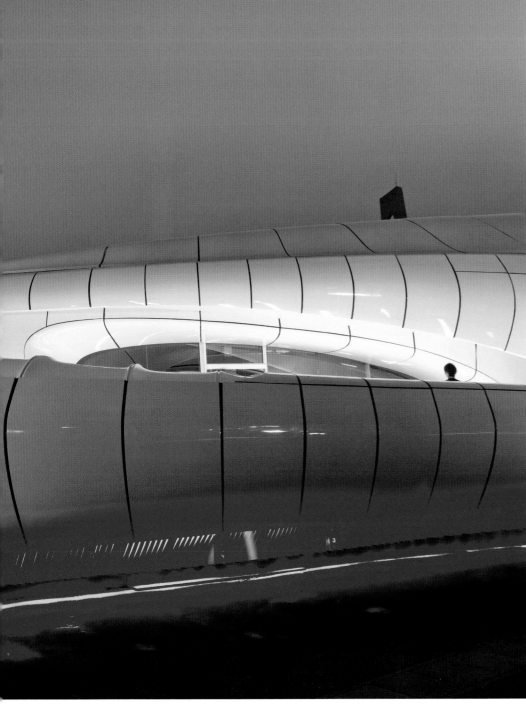

Left A traveling art museum, Chanel Mobile Art, seems perfectly situated in its temporary Tokyo location in Olympic Plaza next to the striking architecture of Yoyogi National Stadium.
Below left A young visitor zips across a rare snowfall in Yoyogi Park.

Below A close look at the bridge to Yoyogi National Stadium reveals a judo bas-relief.

Left "Gothic Lolitas" hang out before an indoor concert at Shibuya Hall.
Below left A gardener gives careful attention to the delicate flowers in the Iris Garden at Meiji Shrine.
Below center The stone plaza surrounding Yoyogi National Stadium is both classic and modern.
Below right A homeless man sleeps on a straw mat in a relatively dry spot under a pedestrian bridge in Yoyogi Park during the rainy season.
Right A mass of young music fans gather for a concert at Yoyogi Park.

Omotesando

In the low city, professions were originally located by edict. High-city professions were place-located, and still are. Take the high-city triangle of Aoyama, Omotesando, and Harajuku. They are adjacent and look alike, all three being resolutely non-trad modern, yet each has its own characteristics.

These have been described by Stephen Mansfield: "Tokyo has fashion towns to match all age brackets: Ginza for the well-heeled, middle-aged, the genteel elderly and the young with mature tastes; Harajuku for off-the-rack teenage costumery; Shibuya is where low-twenties catwalk wannabes gather; Aoyama is for the high-brand sartorially conscious shopper," and Omotesando advertises itself as having "world-class design, elegant cuisine, and cosmopolitan café culture."

These latter claims are backed by the main Omotesando avenue's now calling itself the Champs-Elysées of Tokyo. This stretch is relatively recent as well as fairly short. It was constructed in 1920 to serve as the major access to the Meiji Shrine, and did not become fashionable until the 1964 Tokyo Olympics lent it some charm.

Omotesando (the name means "Front Approach," referring to entry into the Shrine) had long been a "good" address, perhaps because of the proximity of the shrine itself. It was along this Champs-Elysées look-alike that one of the places deemed fashionable to live was constructed in the optimistic aftermath of the 1923 Kanto earthquake.

These were the *Donjunkai* apartments, the first-multi-housing project in Japan. Bauhaus-inspired, they were opened in 1927 and soon became fashionable as well as famous. They did not last, but then nothing lasts in Tokyo as it is so much cheaper to rebuild than it is to conserve.

Destroyed in 2006, their place was taken by a new complex. Smartly named Omotesando Hills after the attention-getting Roppongi Hills complex (same development company), it may contain many less apartments (only 38) but holds many more shops (some 130).

It also projects the illusion of cutting-edge modernity, a quality that has been cherished in Japan for centuries, beginning with vogues for the new still evident in Edo history and before. *Iki*, that Edo talisman pointing to the ideals of the urban commoner, pointing toward (says the dictionary) "an urbane, chic, bourgeois type of beauty with undertones of sensuality," is still much with us in Omotesando.

One needn't wait long for fashionable people to bicycle by Louis Vuitton's flagship on trendy Omotesando Avenue, known to some as Tokyo's Champs-Elysees.

Above left Omotesando Hills is a fairly recent addition to the area's fashion boutique line-up.
Above The large traditional stone lantern that marks the way to Meiji Shrine stands amidst streaking traffic and advertising billboards on Aoyama Avenue.
Left A young woman vacuums stairs inside Emporio Armani on Omotesando Avenue.

Below right (from left to right) A Ralph Lauren staffer sweeps up in front of the store on Omotesando Avenue. Autumn leaves and sunshine make the wide sidewalks of Omotesando a great place to stroll. Huge advertisements serve as a changing backdrop along Omotesando Avenue. Bare winter trees reflect in the Tod's Building, by architect Toyo Ito.

Harajuku

As we move west across megacity Tokyo, people seem to become younger. The low city looks older and grayer now, but in the high city there appear to be more adolescents and young adults than ever. And no place is, in this sense, more juvenile than Harajuku.

A part of what has been called the "shopping triangle," Harajuku was also the last of the high-city sections to develop its own personality. It was originally simply a rural station (the name has been rendered "meadow lodging") until the 1964 Oympics cast its glamour on the area and made it an attractive site for merchandising.

Just as old Edo insisted that different classes live in different places, so contemporary Tokyo even now insists upon a like differentiation. The affluent young, even if they do not live in the shopping triangle, must often visit it. This is where the latest fashions are to be discovered or invented. This is their place to shop.

Most of the youthful fashion-passions originate in the Shibuya/Harajuku area. Their most public venues are in tiny, crowded Takeshita Street, and around Harajuku Station on the continuation of Omotesando Avenue. Here the young converge.

Here too is the site of one of the most dramatic confrontations between old and new in megacity Tokyo. At the very heart of the fashionable frenzy,

with crowds of teeny-boppers strutting about and proclaiming a mercantile future for us all, suddenly looms the mighty *torii* gateway, backed by the great silent forest and the hushed antiquity of Meiji Shrine.

Though it is not all that old (Meiji died in 1912, and his shrine was dedicated in 1920, only to be destroyed by the airraids of 1945 and not rebuilt until 1958), the great shrine and its seemingly ancient forest—seventy acres of it—its great lake of iris, the hushed strains of sacred *kagura* dancing, of *gagaku* court-music, speak of age,

Above Hip young women staff the clothing boutiques targeting youth along Takeshita Street.
Right A young woman relaxes in a café overlooking Harajuku Station and the greenery of Meji Shrine.

veneration, respect, restriction: all of these things most foreign to the cavorting young just outside the gate—a true graphic contrast between old and now, low city and high city, history and the present.

Far left Rain accentuates the somber mood of Meiji Shrine's central sanctuary where *Kannushi* (Shinto priests) all carry umbrellas.
Near left *Kannushi* and *Miko* (Shrine Maidens) conduct a ceremony inside the Outer Shrine.
Left bottom A lone visitor crosses the Meiji Shrine's central sanctuary.
Right (from top to bottom) Visitors pause respectfully in the rainy central sanctuary. *Kannushi* and *Miko* proceed through an alcove for a ceremony inside the Outer Shrine. A large *torii* gate of *hinoki* (cypress) wood with the Imperial Chrysanthemum Crest stands at the entrance to the Meiji Shrine's central sanctuary. A young girl in traditional kimono seems torn between multiple cameras.

Above left A young woman wears a literal fashion statement.

Above center Shop staff wear colorful kimono to attract shoppers.

Above right Stylish young women wait to cross Omotesando Avenue in the heart of Harajuku.

Left A cute shopgirl greets customers on Meiji Avenue.

Right That modern fashion accessory, the cellphone, is also handy for coordinating one's schedule and keeping in touch with one's friends.

Ebisu

Just as Harajuku owes its economic and hence social importance to merchandising, so Ebisu is another area created by product demand.

As a community it was founded late, around 1928, because of the needs of a single concern: the Japan Beer Brewery Company. Though the beverage had been in production since 1890, more space was now required for its fermentation, and was thus the area was named after the beer itself: Ebisu.

This, in turn, was the name of one of the local gods, a member of the *Shichifukujin,* the seven deities of good fortune, Chinese imports all. Ebisu is the deity of prosperity, and hence of use to a struggling young beer company. Shortly, the product itself was given the god's name (Yebisu, a purposely archaic spelling used to suggest probity), and prosperity has duly ensued.

One of the results was the earliest of the mega complexes that now cram megacity Tokyo. This is Yebisu Garden Place, an enormous multiplex which features a tower, a hotel, a real French restaurant in a faux chateau, a museum or two, a covered moving walkway to get there from the station, and, of course, an historical gallery of beer and a number of beer halls.You knew where you were as soon as you stepped off the train. All Japanese railways stations have different musical themes, broadcast when trains come and go. And what was

the theme for Ebisu? The Yebisu beer TV commercial jingle, of course. Then perhaps someone complained. It is now that zither melody from *The Third Man*.

With such a complex as the Yebisu beer people developed giving new importance to an otherwise undistinguished area, it is understandable that a number of enterprises grew in its shadow, and not surprising that many of these are eating and drinking places.

Ebisu is known for its restaurant life, from the stand-and-drink stalls (*tachinomi*) to Japanese-style *izakaya*, to "English" and "Irish" pubs, to a full panoply of ethnic eateries, and pricier victuals available in the upper reaches of the Garden Place Tower.

Above Yebisu Garden Place's Central Square is partially covered by a sweeping glass canopy.
Above right A young woman relaxes in the sunny cafe of the Tokyo Metropolitan Museum of Photography at Yebisu Garden Place.

Right And, of course, a Chateau! Well, the Chateau Restaurant Taillvent-Robuchon anyway.

Opposite top A *yatai* (food stall) near Ebisu Station offers *oden* (steamed dishes), cold beer, and hot saké.

Above Zest Cantina has a relaxed atmosphere and a Tex-Mex menu.

Far left A sparkling taxi with uniformed driver stops beneath an imposing mural of the Buddha.

Middle left Traditional *hanko* (name seals) form a complex pattern outside a stationary shop.

Near left Generations meet at the ornamental fountain in the Central Square plaza at Yebisu Garden Place.

Right A smiling Ebisu-san, God of Wealth, sits outside Ebisu Station.

Shibuya

As the high city climbed ever higher, and the city limits reached out even further, two new centers emerged, both to mature into cities within the city: Shibuya and Shinjuku.

The former was among the low hills of the southwest, and in the early Meiji years was known mainly for the wonderful quality of its tea. The elegant residential area which is now Shoto used to be a tea plantation.

Shibuya was originally open countryside, but already had its own railway station in 1885 when the Yamanote Line that encircles high-city Tokyo was opened.

It was already on a major crossroad, and this easy access brought in first the military, which had early drilling grounds here. The military made room for the mercantile after the place was incorporated as village in 1889 and as a town in 1909. Though damaged by the Great Kanto Earthquake of 1923, it had recovered sufficiently to be called Shibuya City by 1932 and was deemed a Tokyo ward in 1947.

The new Shibuya is the "center of youth culture and youth fashion," with its brand awareness and endless shopping, where, according to a one advertisement, "the person you pass is beautiful."

Transient fashion industries grew during the late 1980s and early 1990s, fueled by an inflated economy. There was not much past to remember and most of it was hidden away in place names.

The major street leading from the station is called *Dogenzaka* (Dogen's Hill). It is now where fashion is made and sold, but it is named after a famous Edo thug, Owada Dogen, who robbed people traveling through Shibuya and then disappeared up the hill.

Occasionally, however, the past could be fabricated. This seems the case with the faithful dog Hachiko, a beast that for years purportedly waited daily at the station for its deceased master.

Now in front of the dog's statue thousands daily wait for each other, the canine monument having become one of the major meeting places in crowded, confusing Tokyo.

Here, amid the juvenile throng, one clearly sees that the place belongs to the young and that Shibuya is just as securely devoted to their interests as ever was old Asakusa or Edo's Ryogoku Bridge.

Youth and fashion intersect at Dogenzaka Crossing, surrounded by advertising billboards in the heart of Shibuya.

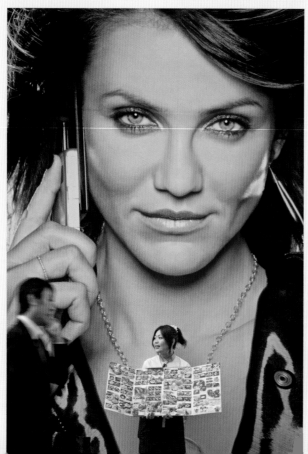

Above Pedestrians swirl past a snap-shooter at the famous "scramble crossing" in front of Shibuya Station.
Right A young pub employee seeks customers the old-fashioned way on the street below a huge cellphone advertisement.

Opposite top The new Shibuya subway station—dubbed "Chichusen, Underground Spaceship," by architect Tadao Ando—features a vast oval-shaped three-story structure that functions as a natural ventilation system, incorporating the airflow created by moving trains to save electricity and reduce carbon dioxide.

Opposite bottom
Commuters and shoppers await an arriving Fukutoshin Line subway train in the Chichusen.

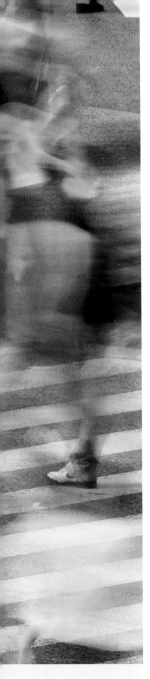

Far left A "velo-taxi" mixes with four-wheeled traffic at Shibuya Crossing.
Near left A momentary matrix of commerce, music and motion is created inside Shibuya Station.

Below left Multi-floor escalators connect the overhead passageways of train stations at Mark City.

Below right A bicyclist glides across a colorful pavement, unusually free of pedestrians and traffic, outside Shibuya Station.

Shinjuku

Originally merely a section of Yotsuya, Shinjuku was a typically somnolent western suburb of Edo. Eventually, however, it woke up enough to serve as one of the stations on the way to Kyoto (it was on the *Koshu Kaido* highway) and to receive a name of its own: New ("*shin*") Station ("*juku*").

The place was originally mostly occupied by the Naito *daimyo,* a part of whose land has now become one of Tokyo's nicest parks, Shinjuku Gyoen. Most of the space, however, eventually was "developed" into one of the busiest sections of Tokyo.

It was, however, a slow starter. Fifty years ago, a municipal reservoir was where all the skyscrapers now stand, and from Shinjuku Station one could enjoy the croaking of frogs at night.

Now, however, the frogs are long departed. The JR Shinjuku Station is the busiest in the world (nearly four million passengers daily pass through it, with 200 exits to help them along).

Instead, where the reservoir used to be, stands the Tokyo Tocho, the mighty Metropolitan Government complex, designed by architect Tange Kenzo, finished in 1990, 45 stories high, and with an unobstructed view of Mt, Fuji. It looks like something from Fritz Lang's film, *Metropolis,* and indeed Shinjuku did inspire another fantastic film. Ridley Scott came, looked around, went home, and made *Blade Runner.*

But it is not only pricey towers. There is an area of bars at the west exit which enjoys the soubriquet of Piss Alley, there is the mini-labyrinth of Golden Gai, a maze of places to drink which has been often slated for "development" but has so far managed to survive.

The most spectacular of these survivals is the area just south of the station, known as Kabuki-cho. It was so named when, postwar, the area was slated for gentrification and a new Kabuki theatre was envisioned.

Now the only theatrical events take place in the largest clutch of motion picture theaters in Tokyo, the ubiquitous strip shows, the voyeur boxes, and the liveliest of street scenes.

Kabuki-cho is an apt place name, however, because here it is possible to see what Edo was like at its most ebulient. Bright, noisy, common, vulgar, beautiful, and very much alive, Tokyo here provides continuity with its past.

Exceptionally clear winter twilight frames Mt. Fuji's distinctive peak rising dramatically in the distance beyond the twinkling skyscrapers of Shinjuku.

Above left Cocoon Tower reflects surrounding high-rise buildings.
Above right Office workers are reflected in a mirrored ceiling of the Shinjuku L Tower as they pass the Cocoon Tower.

Left A sculpture is silhouetted in Citizen's Plaza at Tokyo City Hall.
Right Commuter trains cross over Yasukuni Avenue traffic, with building-size posters as a seamless backdrop.

Opposite top Cherry blossoms bloom overhead and lie underfoot at Shinjuku Gyoen.
Opposite middle Visitors relax in late afternoon sunlight in a secluded corner of the gardens.
Opposite bottom Pubs of all types, from the funky to the refined, can be found in Kabukicho after dark.

Above Shinjuku Gyoen is a very popular destination for school daytrips.
Left A painter is inspired by the natural colors of spring blossoms along a garden pond.

Afterword

The world's largest city and one of its most livable, Tokyo is a combination of attributes and attitudes which, despite the massive size of the place, fit the slender human frame well.

Just as modern Tokyo is undergirded by old Edo, so too this city in other ways looks radical but remains traditional. It combines the new and the old, the modern and traditional, the trendy and the timeless. Well, what city doesn't? True, but Tokyo does it in its own singular fashion.

It has been said that this city is where the festival dragon and the everyday auto lie down together, where the priest strikes his morning temple bell by the time-tone coming in over his clock radio, where a far flung mega-metropolis remains a cluster of simple villages, and skyscrapers are built on land that still shakes.

Maybe these are among the things that constitute Tokyo's frenetic, kitsch-ridden, crowd-friendly style. At first hurried, harried, and distracted, but at second glance it seems no such thing. The traveler would be tempted to echo Henry James' words on London: "The city has no style, only innumerable attempts to style."

Air of the new, scent of the old—a more or less contented people walk around wearing i-pods, examining their cell phones as though they were breviaries. They use plastic cards for just about everything, but they wait for traffic lights. They gather in buzzing, buying swarms but they relish the single experience—the solitary view from Tokyo Tower, the song lyric like a haiku.

And the Tokyo person resides in the greatest emporium in the world: durian, bidets, mangoes, slivovitz, Demal chocolates galore, and the complete works of Webern on CD. Consumerism gone mad is indeed the Tokyo way of life.

And everything works, from the phones to the subways to the humble vending machines. These disperse one thousand new types of drinks every year, and there are over 400,000 of these machines in Tokyo, one for every 20 people. If there is a magnitude seven earthquake, and estimated 39,000 machines will topple over.

Holding this sprawling, vibrant place together is the finest public transportation system in the world, one of the best reasons that Tokyo is among the most livable cities. Imagine trying to live in this mega-monster without it.

The system holds major elevated train lines, an elaborate subway system, a full bus system, a couple of monorails, lots of elevators and escalators, an enormous fleet of taxis, and a single tram.

Tokyo's major train lines consist of a circle line and two lines that cut through it. The circle is the Yamanote Line, a loop 34.5 kms

The old well still pumps water at the flower shop for visitors to Zoshigaya Cemetery.

The sprawling lights of Megacity Tokyo surround visitors atop Tokyo Tower Observatory.

(21.5 miles) in circumference, along which are 29 stations, not counting that one between Harajuku and Yoyogi, now perpetually closed and intended for the exclusive use of the Imperial family during the 1964 Olympic Games.

Although the Yamanote loop has no terminal, many of its stops connect with subway lines crossing Tokyo, and/or private train lines to transport the commuter from central Tokyo out to the surrounding suburbs.

It takes just over an hour to go around the loop (walking, it has been estimated, would take twelve hours), and there are a total of 667 runs every day. During peak hours trains run 2.5 minutes apart.

The tracks cutting through the circle are the Keihin-Tohoku Line, which runs from Saitama in the north to Yokohama in the south and beyond, and the Sobu/Chuo line which runs east to west through the low city (and before that the neighboring prefecture of Chiba) to the high city (Shinjuku and beyond). These are the main commuter lines into the suburbs.

There are well over two million commuters squeezing daily into Tokyo proper from Greater Tokyo, each taking an average of seventy minutes each way—making up an aggregate journey of 614 person-years a day. Over a 45-year career, each commuter would spend nearly three years traveling to and from work.

Tokyo is famously the city where rush-hour pushers are employed to shove passengers into already packed trains, an experience during which losing a shoe is not at all uncommon. Nonetheless, trains almost always depart and arrive on time, and even a minute's delay results in profuse apologies.

Equally punctual is the city's vast subway system. There are 13 lines, making it the third longest in the world, after those of London and New York. Like the London underground, the Tokyo subway trains are color coded and, like the Paris system, each train is designated by its terminal.

There are maps both in the cars and on the platforms listing where you are and where you want to go. There are also electronic indicators within the cars, all stations are also locatable by a numeral system, and the whole things is bilingual (Japanese-English), so that it is almost impossible to get lost, tangle though Tokyo is.

The first subway, running the two kilometers between Asakusa and Ueno, opened in 1927, and what has been described as the last, the Fukutoshin Line, operating between Shibuya and Ikebukuro and beyond, opened in 2008.

The deepest station is Roppongi on the Oedo line, which lies more than 42 meters below the surface. It is consequently designated one of the safest in the event of an earthquake, though users have noticed that they seem to spend more time on the escalators up and down than they do in the subway car itself.

The bus system, which runs just about everywhere in Tokyo, is not quite so convenient to the visitor as are the train and subway systems, but the destinations are now appearing in romanized script (i.e., "English") on front and back of the vehicle. The several monorails (the most famous being that which connects Haneda Airport to the rest of Tokyo) are easy to use, as are the many elevators. The longest of the equally many escalators is found in Ikebukuro's Metropolitan Art Space, and the shortest (83.4 cm / 2 ft. 8 in.) is not even in the capital but at a shopping mall in Kawasaki, between Tokyo and Yokohama.

In addition there are the taxi cabs, so ubiquitous that they can be hailed on any street. There are some 80,000 drivers working for the taxi companies and an addition 20,000 drivers of private ("white") taxis.

This enormous transportation system is necessary to move Tokyo people around their massive city. An added complication is that, as we have seen, Tokyo has no center. Or, says philosopher Roland Barthes, "Tokyo does possess a center but that center is empty."

Home of the squirrel, the badger, and the Imperial family, the Imperial Palace none the less does not function as a city-center, nor do any of the other major nodes on the transportation belts. Barthes continues: "Reticulated cities (Los Angeles, for instance) are said to produce a profound uneasiness: they offend our synesthetic sentiment of The City, which requires that any urban space has a center to go to, to return from."

While agreeing that Los Angeles can generate profound uneasiness, one wonders if being reticulated (that is, being made in a pattern of interlacing lines, like a net or a network) has much to do with it. Art critic Hunter Drohojowska would think not. "It is natural," she writes, "for anyone who likes Los Angeles to love Tokyo . . . in both places citizens value the interplay of surface, are unabashedly comfortable with artificiality, and in both places shopping has been elevated to an art form."

Also, module Tokyo (same structures in the "village," same villages in the ward, same wards in the city, with each major node on the travel wheel—Ueno, Shinjuku, Shibuya, Shinagawa— becoming a city-within-the-city in its own right) fits the Tokyo dweller very well.

Perhaps also the Japanese tend, more openly than most people, to avail themselves of the advantages of module "thinking." This way of thought (make units of everything, reduce everything to bite-size pieces) distinguishes all Japanese domestic architecture (old and new), where my *tatami* mat or my new plastic bathroom shell are interchangeable with yours. It informs most teaching processes: Japanese dance, the martial arts, much else—all are taught in the form of modules called *kata*.

Such modular thinking is also economically advantageous. It lowers unit cost. What is now true of computer parts and precast bathrooms was once true of *tatami* sizes and remains true of seasonal compliments.

In the Japanese language, thought itself tends to modular form—so do all languages but not to this extent and not so

A springtime scene of in the garden of *Koishikawa Korakuen*.

The elegantly illuminated steel girder construction of Tokyo Tower shines above a sparkling maze-like grid of city streets at twilight.

apparently. Here the ritual is really observed and the cliché is truly respected. So much so that foreigners often criticize Japanese for being ant-like, robot-like—everyone doing the same thing, thinking the same thoughts.

This is obviously true of no people and it is equally untrue of the Japanese. Novelist Shiba Ryotaru has explained why. "The notion that we Japanese all share the same values is a gross oversimplification. Creative thinking and social activism are the products of a society that honors pluralistic values. Each of the almost three hundred feudal domains into which Japan was divided boasted an individuality and a diversity all of its own."

Perhaps the confusion occurs because Japan is doubly endowed. There is a personal self, and there is a social self as well. This is true all over the world, but Japan exhibits them side by side and considers them of equal importance, attempting to hide neither. The citizen, like the city, is left unzoned. One is both oneself and also a member of a strongly knit social fabric. The rich man's mansion and the poor man's shack abut. Trad and mod back each other up.

One result is a people more openly inured to playing the double role of a single person and also a lifelong member of a strict society. There is the conflict typified by *giri-ninjo* where *giri* (social duty) wars against *ninjo* (personal inclination). There is accord when one manicures one's own garden but throws the discovered dead cat over the wall and into the public street.

All of this is open, visible, appreciable. Japan is said to be private and even secretive, but nothing could be so frontal as this unthinking display of double allegiance—to society and to self. It is palpable and, as we have seen, in Tokyo it takes concrete form.

One result is a city made for everybody. It never had any such intention, but the result is a very alive, vibrant, exciting city—spectacularly livable, friendly to those who can afford it, and cold to those (the local homeless, the indigent refugee, the poor backpacker) who cannot, a big smile for the insider, a big frown for the outsider.

Where can it go from now as we float down the drain of history? It is already a mega city and Japan itself is showing signs of being one megopolis, extending from Tokyo all the way down to Fukuoka in Kyushu.

But this is perhaps not the best question to ask about a place which has long been formed through natural, organic structure, and not (or not entirely) by the bumbling hand of man, where *ninjo* nevertheless rarely trumps *giri*.

There may be, as Lafcadio Hearn believed, no Japan like Tokyo. But this enormous city, sitting like a tumor on a corpse or like a brain on a body, incorporates within itself a place created by its many citizens, by these millions of individuals, and not (or not entirely) by the government, the warlords, the captains of industry, or the developers.

Sources

Abe Kobo, *The Dead Girl's Song*, (Shinda Musume ga Utatta), (Tokyo, 1954)

Angles, J. and Rimer, J. Thomas (eds.), *Japan: A Traveller's Literary Companion*, (Berkeley, 2006)

Anon., *The Hidden Order: Tokyo through the Twentieth Century*, (Tokyo 1989)

____, 'The Big 600,' *Metropolis*, Issue 500, Sept. 23, 2005

____, 'Let's Get Trivial,' *Metropolis*, Issue 601, Sept. 30, 2005

____, 'Population of Tokyo,' *Japan Times*, 15 Feb. 1998

____, 'Tokyo: A Livable Megacity' *Japan Times*, 30 June 2008

____, 'Tokyo's Vulnerability Exposed,' *Japan Times*, 16 January 1998

Ashihara Yoshinobu, *The Aesthetic Townscape* (Cambridge, 1983)

Barthes, Roland, *Empire of Signs* (Paris,1970; New York, 1982)

Bestor, Theodore, *Neighborhood Tokyo* (Stanford, 1989)

Betros, Chris, 'On the Move,' (*Metropolis*, Issue 741, June 6, 2008

Bird, Isabella, *Unbeaten Tracks in Japan* (New York: 1880; reprint, Tokyo, 1984)

Chesterton, G.K., *What I Saw in America* (London, 1923)

Curzon, George, *Tales of Travel* (London, 1923)

Drohojowska, Hunter, *The View from the South* (*California*, June, 1989)

Edo/Tokyo Museum Foundation, *Guide to Edo/Tokyo Museum* (Tokyo, 1995)

Girouard, Mark, *Cities and People* (New Haven, 1985)

Graves, William, 'Tokyo,' *The National Geographic* (November, 1986)

Griffes, W.E., *The Mikado's Empire* (New York, 1876; reprinted, 1976)

Guest, Harry. ed., *Traveller's Literary Companion: Japan* (Brighton, 1994)

James, Henry, *Essays on London and Elsewhere* (London, 1893)

Jinnai Hidenobu, Tokyo: *A Spatial Anthropology* (Berkeley, 1995)

Kami Ryusuke, Tokyo: *Sights and Insights* (Toyo, 1992)

Kawabata, Yasunari, *The Crimson Band of Asakusa* (Asakusa Kurenaidan) (Tokyo, 1930/ Berkeley, 2005)

Karan, P., and Stapleton, K,(eds.), *The Japanese City* (Lexington, KY 1997)

Kawaguchi, Judit, 'Words to Live By,' *The Japan Times*, Sept. 23, 2008.

Krupat, Edward, *People in Cities* (Cambridge, 1986)

Lee O-Young, *The Compact Culture* (Tokyo, 1984)

Lees, Andrew, *Cities Perceived* (Manchester, 1986)

Lowell, Percival, *The Soul of the Far East* (New York, 1888)

Maki Fumihiko (ed.). *Glimpses of a Hidden City* (Mie Gakure Suru Toshi), (Tokyo, 1980)

Mansfield, Stephen, 'Tokyo: Epicenter of Brand,' *Tokyo Journal*, No. 26, Summer, 2008

Markus, Andrew. 'The Carnival of Edo' (Cambridge: *The Harvard Journal*, 1985)

Michaux, Henri, *A Barbarian in Asia* (Paris, 1945: New York, 1949)

Mumford, Lewis, *The City in History* (London, 1961)

Nagai Kafu, *During the Rains* (Tsuyu no Atosaki) (Tokyo, 1931; New York, 1994)

Nishiyama Matsunosuke, *Edo Culture* (Honolulu: Univ. of Hawai'i Press, 1997)

Norman, Henry, *The Real Japan* (New York, 1892)

Olsen, Donald, *The City as a Work of Art* (New Haven, 1986)

Pons, Philippe, *D'Edo à Tokyo* (Paris, 1988)

Popham, Peter, Tokyo: *The City at the End of the World* (Tokyo, 1985)

Quennell, Peter, *A Superficial Journey through Tokyo and Peking* (Londn, 1932)

Richie, Donald, *Introducing Tokyo* (Tokyo, 1987)

_____, *A Lateral View* (Tokyo, 1991)

_____, Notes for a Study on Shohei Imamura, (Toronto, 1997)

_____, *Partial Views* (Tokyo, 1995)

_____, 'Tokyo,' (*Orient-East*, Tokyo 1960)

_____, Tokyo: *A View of the City* (London, 1999)

_____, 'Walking in Tokyo,' in Tokyo: *Form and Spirit,* New York, 1986)

Riesman, David, *Conversations with Japan* (New York, 1967)

Said, Edward, *Orientalism* (New York, 1978)

Sancton, Thomas, 'Tokyo: Inside the Super City,' *Time*, 5 May 1986

Seidensticker, Edward, *Kafu the Scribbler* (Stanford, 1965)

_____, *Low City, High City* (New York, 1983)

_____, *Tokyo Rising* (New York, 1990)

Sennett, Richard, *Flesh and Stone* (New York, 1994)

Siebald, Phillipp, *Manners and Customs of the Japanese* (London, 1841; Tokyo, 1973)

Singer, Kurt, *Mirror, Sword and Jewel* (London, 1973)

Smith, Henry, *Edo-Tokyo Gaku Josetsu* (Tokyo, 1985)

Taito Ward Board of Education, *The Shitamachi Museum* (Tokyo, 1983)

Takashina Shuji (ed.), 'Tokyo: Creative Chaos,' *Japan Echo*, Tokyo, 1986)

Tange Kenzo, 'Tokyo-Its Past and Future,' *Japan Times*, 4-5 January, 1987

Tanizaki, Jun'ichiro, *Childhood Years* (Yoshi Jidai) (Tokyo, 1956; Tokyo 1988)

_____, *Diary of a Mad Old Man* (Futen Roji Nikki) (Tokyo, 1962; New York, 1965)

Thwaite, Anthony, 'Tokyo: A Jumbled, Confused City,' *Asahi Evening News*, 26 March 1986

Thomson, J.M., *Great Cities and their Traffic* (London, 1978)

Tokyo Metropolitan Government, *Tokyo Life* (1996)

Waley, Paul, Tokyo: *City of Stories* (Tokyo, 1991)

_____. *Tokyo Now and Then* (Tokyo, 1984)

Ward, Philip, *Japanese Capitals* (Cambridge, 1985)

Yazaki, Takeo, *The Japanese City* (Tokyo, 1963)

Below left A young girl in kimono poses with striking confidence at Meiji Shrine.
Below right A young woman checks her cellphone while riding her bicycle past an old 1950's black-and-white mural of Nihonbashi Bridge.